Nuts,
Bolts,
and
Gut-Level Management

Gordon A. Shave

PARKER PUBLISHING COMPANY, INC.
WEST NYACK, NEW YORK

© 1974, *by*

PARKER PUBLISHING COMPANY, INC.
West Nyack, New York

Library of Congress Cataloging in Publication Data

Shave, Gordon A
  Nuts, bolts, and gut-level management.

  Report of extended discussions with R. F. Babbidge.
  1. Management. I. Babbidge, Robert F. II. Title.
HD31.S433   658.4   74-8439
ISBN 0-13-627844-2

Printed in the United States of America

FOREWORD

by Dr. John R. VandeWater

A key problem in management was depicted in a magazine cartoon which featured a harried executive putting down the telephone. The caption said it all: "What interruption was I working on when I was last interrupted?"

The manager was a typical "fire-fighter," wrapped up in job detail, moving from crisis to crisis with no discretionary time, no analysis of his priorities, and little freedom to create or innovate.

If I were asked what makes a manager a true professional I would reply that he would be a creative person—not locked in on the "tried and proven." He'd be rational in his problem discovery and problem solving and would know how to implement and follow through an effective correction. He would be goal oriented, deeply concerned with planning and setting priorities, and possessed of a strong inner desire for achieving results. He would have and practice a code of ethics and believe that service to society was a paramount concern.

Equally important, he would be able to apply the full

9

body of his knowledge, knowing that it is not enough to organize, staff, plan, direct and control unless he has a complete system to bring his subordinates into the fold of his expertise.

Mr. Robert Babbidge, about whom this book is written, years ago recognized these areas of need which have only recently attracted expert attention. He saw from his own experience that many ideas, policies and procedures were given in management development programs which never saw expression on the manager's job station.

He recognized the need for a manager to have his own planned management program, to develop supportive job procedures for and with his subordinates, and to establish his own Operating Letter system in which detailed action steps could be outlined.

More than this, he sensed a need for a better system to record, process and execute the many projects a manager sees from day to day, and a method for inspecting results after implementation, so that all personnel could be aided in their work and held realistically accountable for the effective use of their time.

He avoided any method that would put an additional burden on the manager or increase the amount of paperwork he handled. He was looking for a means to free him and his subordinates from all confusion that wastes time year after year.

This book sets forth the results of twenty years of his experimentation. It describes a system usable by any manager who longs to do a more effective job regardless of whether his work is related to commercial, industrial, hospital, educational administration, government, or voluntary association activities.

With this system to help him, any manager can take new information he may learn or has learned in the past from any management development program and put every bit of his knowledge into immediate application at his and his subordinates' job stations.

It is my belief that this book will help you meet the tests

of effective management in action every minute of the day and every day of your career.

The author, Gordon A. Shave, an effective management consultant in his own right, uses a compelling, discursive style to bring the reader a lively, interesting and practical definition of Mr. Babbidge's system. Mr. Shave is a competent journalist with a highly diversified business background. He combines the art of writing with a candid probing technique which has produced some dialogue that should have been written many years ago. The book will unquestionably represent a substantial increase in your inventory of competence, and should be read by every manager and every student of the management profession.

A word
from
the author

Once in probably half a century something happens in the science of management that parallels the dramatic beneficence of the great happenings in medicine. It receives less public acclaim, of course, because it touches the imagination of only a small segment of the population. Yet, for those it does touch it could have no less an impact on their personal lives—their health, happiness, affluence—than would the discovery of insulin, polio vaccine, or a cure for cancer have on the victims of these diseases.

The management system described in this book will be for you, the manager, or you, the student of management, a veritable elixir for job station proficiency and personal happiness, no less significant than any discovery in any discipline that has preceded it.

Here are just a few of the incredible benefits this system can provide for you:

- Night-time and weekend work loads will stop.
- Replacement of valuable employees will be routine.
- Management by controlled intention will be normal.
- Things will be done correctly the first time and every time after that.
- Promotions will be earned and will appear to be earned.
- Reports will be done accurately and on time.
- Projects will be completed.
- Creativeness will be expanded and harnessed.
- Reduction in operating costs is virtually guaranteed.
- Contentment at job stations will characterize the work force.

The list could go on. In fact, you will find the answer to every negative phase in the management function between these two covers.

This is the first book published that brings the system to your attention. It describes an interview I had with Robert F. Babbidge, one of the authors of *The Four Basic Management and Administrative Procedure Systems,* during which he turned me from a first class skeptic about the fantastic things I had heard about the system, into an out-and-out disciple and practitioner.

You are in for a delightful surprise if you have ever entertained the idea that there are no answers for the problems of managing. There *are* answers, and twenty years of development and experimentation have proven them—and they are all inside this book.

Gordon A. Shave

TABLE
OF
CONTENTS

Foreword 9

A Word from the Author 12

1. How to Take Adversity in Stride—and Turn It to
   Your Advantage 23

   Coping with an Emergency 26

2. How to Keep Your Division Functioning During
   an Emergency 29

   Amazing Efficiency 32

3. Setting Up a System That Frees You from "Traffic
   Cop" Managing 33

An Administrative Discovery 36
Overcoming Problems of Personnel Changes . . 36
With a Planned Management Program to Use,
    Even a Novice Could Take Over the Boss's
    Administrative Tasks 37
Scheduling Activities 38
Setting Up a Calendar 38
If You Don't Know Accountability from
    Responsibility You Are in Deep Trouble. . .a
    "Do-It-Yourselfer" Is Not a Competent
    Manager. Delegate but Don't Abdicate 40
Filing Work Force Reports 40
Wage Costs Should Influence Delegation
    Decisions 41
How Abdication Can Perpetuate "Job
    Training" 41
How to Delegate 42
The Blackmailed Boss Is a Cinch to Crack
    under the Strain. . .with J. P.'s Everyone
    Can Be Replaced 43
The Critical Test of a System Comes When a
    Subordinate Takes Over Your Job Station . . 44

4. **How to Vastly Increase Your Discretionary Time** 45

How to Stop the New-Hire from Devouring
    Your Time 48
Counting Up the Time Involved 49
In-Office "Baby Sitting" Can Be Stopped 49
How to Set Priorities. . .Handle a Crisis. . .and
    Have Time Left Over 50
Re-organizing Priorities 51
A Change in the Plan 52
Returning to Routine 52
Knowing Precisely What Has to Be Done 53

A Matter of Control 54
How to Analyze a Job into Component Parts
   and Get the Whole Picture 55
Looking at the Parts 55
Chipping Away at Responsibilities 56
How to Eliminate 90% of Your
   Accountabilities 57
How to Change an "Empire Builder" into a
   Proficient Manager 58
Dealing with Redundancy 59

5. How to Make a System Do What You Force
   Your Memory to Do. . .and Do It Better 61

Changing Managerial Functions 64
Finding a Memory Substitute 65
Making Room for Creative Work 67
Handling Hundreds of Different Assignments . 68
Using People in More Productive Ways 69
How Job Details Are Remembered 70

   How to Remember Procedure Details
   Forever

How P.M.P. Provides Freedom 72
Using Time Effectively 73
How to Make Your Subordinate Responsible
   for Your Promotions 74
Strengthening Management Positions........ 76
Dealing with Constant Change 77
How to Avoid Wasted Training 78
How to Convert Classroom Knowledge to
   Job Station Proficiency 79
Applying Managerial Knowledge 80
Using 4BMAP with Other Systems 81

6. How You Can Guarantee Subordinate Efficiency, Involvement and Job Satisfaction 83

What Is the Difference Between a Job
Description and a Job Procedure?

The Shortcomings of Job Descriptions 88

How Your Secretary Can Handle Details
You Think You Should Handle ● Author's
Note ● More Examples

How to Improve or Eliminate Procedures by
"Straight-Line" Thinking............... 93
Handling Variations in Job Functions 93
How to Overcome Resistance to Change and
Get Subordinates Enthused About Job
Enrichment 94
What the Employee Wants from the System .. 95
How to Replace "Redundancy" with
"Potential" 96
How to Make the System Take Over a Job
Vacancy 96
How Job Procedures Lessen Drudgery 97
How to Put a New Employee into Production
in Less Than One Hour 99
How Recorded Procedural Changes Can
Prevent Critical Work Overloads 100

How to Keep the Payroll Stable and
Handle the Work Overload Too

Integrating the Work Flow 103
How to Get Accurate Productivity at Once ... 104
How to Convince an Employee He Is Doing
the Job Exactly As You Want It Done 105

How J. P.'s Reduce Demoralizing Criticism ... 106
How a President Incorrectly Assessed His
    General Manager 107
A New Look at Causes of Economic
    Regressions 108
How 4BMAP Unleashes Talent 109
Using "Foot Motivation" 111

7. **Advantages of the Operating Letter System** 113

    How an Operating Letter Can Turn a Head
    Office Directive into a Job-Station Procedure

How to Avoid "Instruction Errors" in
    Communications   118
How an "Operating Letter" Works   119
How to Examine the Components of a
    Letter or Memo   120
Overcoming the Problems Posed by
    Directives   121
Letters and Memos vs. Systems   122
How to Avoid Negative Results from
    Faulty Communications   123
Interpretation and Confusion   124
How to Guarantee the Effective Trans-
    mission and Reception of Directives   125
How to Create a Vastly Improved
    Retrieval System for All Directives   127
How to Get Your Subordinates Involved   128
How the Operating Letter System Works....   129
The System at the District Level   130
How a Head Office Directive Can Be
    Understood by Every Person in the
    Work Force   131
How to Make a Company Operating Manual
    Work in Your Branch or Department.....   133

Shortcomings of a Company Manual 133
How the Mid-Manager Can Positively
   Guarantee Follow-Up by His
   Subordinates 135
How the Weekly Management Meeting Can
   Become Intensely Productive 137
How Operating Letters Force Action 138
How to Interrelate Your Responsibilities
   with Your Subordinate's
   Accountabilities 139

8. **How to Guarantee the Completion of Every
   Project You Accept or Originate** **141**

How Projects Disappear 144
How to Overcome Survey Problems and
   Save Thousands of Dollars 145
How to Keep Your Project Meeting on
   Target 146
What Happens to Project Assignments 146
How a Project Committee Is Formed 147
How to Get Vertical Cooperation Between
   One Project Committee and Another 148
How to Capture the Creative Input of
   Managers 149
How Participatory Management Can Stop
   Grievances Before They Arise 150
How the System Pays Off 151
Knowing What Workers Want 153
How a Manager's Project Committee Can
   Improve the Working Conditions of an
   Entire Work Group 154
How Project Committees Can Improve
   Working Conditions 155
How to Handle Fifteen Projects in an Hour .. 156

How to Avoid Launching a Project for the
    Second Time 157
How to Keep Committee Effectiveness
    High 158
How the Status Report Eliminates Minutes .. 158
How to Keep Speeches Out of the
    Committee Room 159
How to Get Your Employee Group to Agree
    to Change 160
How Bob Takes "Formal Education" Apart
    and Puts It Back Together 162
How Systems Make Knowledge Operative ... 163
The Difficulty of Implementing........... 164

9. **How the Detailed Job Inspection System Puts It
   All Together** 167

How the 4BMAP System Can Reduce
Executive Turnover ● How the 4BMAP
System Can Provide a Valuable Tool for
Self-Actualization ● The Five Basic Needs
Every Manager Should Understand ● How
Management Has Permitted the Worker to
Switch His Allegiance ● How Participatory
Management Is Often Killed by Those Who
Want It ● Why Job Station Creativeness
Depends on a System as Much as on Talent

How to Take the Sting Out of the Word
    "Inspection" 178
Two Types of Inspection 179

How Inspections Are Frequently Conducted

How the Inspection Method Could Be
    Improved 181
Why the Inspector Needs to Be as Prepared
    as the "Inspected" 182

How to Get Response from the Man
Inspected 183
With the Right System Employees Insist on
Inspections 184
The Opportunity to Show Talent 184
Two Essential Ingredients of Inspection
Success 186
How to Prevent an Inspection from Turning
into a "Witch Hunt" 187
How to Overcome an Inspection Dilemma . . . 187
The Answer to the Dilemma 188
The Role of Labor Representatives 190
How Common Sense Plus Experience Equals
Management Effectiveness 191
The Essential Element 191
How "More Pay for Less Work" Should
Be Analyzed 193
The Problem of Leisure 193
How Managers Have Grown Less Effective . . . 194

How the Employee Group Recognizes
Effective Leadership

How to Find Solutions Rather Than Faults . . 197
How Senior Management Can Handle
Bench-Level Inspections 198
Who Will Make the Final Choice of the
Leader? 199
How Workers Will Choose 200

10. How You Can Use 4BMAP as a "Full Circle"
Management System 203

First Steps in Introducing 4BMAP 206
The Manager's Programming Schedule 207

How to Explain, Introduce, Execute,
Supervise and Inspect ● How the Project
Committee Solves a Problem and What
Happens to the Solution ● How Manage-
ment Directives Can Be "Locked in" ●
Some of the Expertise That Went into
4BMAP ●

Evolution of the System 213
The First Seminar 213

How the Independent Businessman, Professional, Etc., Can Use the System ● How
a University Professor Became an Efficient
Property Manager

11. Five Important Observations Based on Experience .. 217

You Need Have No Fear of Pre-Announcing
Inspections

How Inspections Can Win Men Back to
   You 220
You Can Have Multiple Numbers of Project
   Committees 220
Even School Taxes Might Be Lowered
   Because of 4BMAP 221

How One General Manager Summed It
All Up

ONE

How to take adversity
in stride and turn it
to your advantage

Bob Babbidge, 54, about 6 feet 1 inch, 180 trim pounds, executive, scuba diver, boat fan, water skier, husband and father of one son, is an unbelievably well-organized executive and virtually the personification of relaxation.

He is also the founder of a management procedural system that is destined to be the most dramatic administrative event of this century.

I have interviewed Bob in his home and in his office and have spent enough days with him to test the consistency of his personality and the reality of his composure. On both counts he would pass any test. He is not an actor, and he's too forthright and candid to bother with deceit.

Bob keeps his business life separated from his domestic life but enjoys a high relaxation level in both.

His working day starts at 8:30 a.m., finishes at 5:00 p.m. Somewhere in the half-hour drive to get to his office he shuts down the domestic part of his life and turns on the vocational, and he reverses the process on the way home.

Despite his heavy job responsibilities (he has hundreds of people to manage) he never takes work home, never uses an hour of free time to wrestle with a vocational problem, and doesn't know what it means to fret about job detail.

During one of my interviews in his home the phone rang. He excused himself, answered it, and when he hung up he said, "Well, it looks like we're going to have a strike on Monday." He might just as well have said, "It's going to rain on Monday."

I know of no executive who wouldn't have terminated that interview at that moment. But Bob was the exception. "How about lunch?" he said, and two hours later, the word "strike" had still to find its way into the conversation.

Coping with an Emergency

About a week later, I was again a guest in his beautifully appointed home at Huntington Harbour, California. The strike was still on. I was having a cup of coffee with Mrs. Babbidge; Bob was at the office. It was a Friday.

"Bob has been a little later getting home since the strike started," she said.

"How late?" I asked.

"Oh, about an hour. He leaves an hour earlier in the morning too," she added.

"I suppose he's bringing work home these days," I suggested.

"No, I don't think it's that bad. In fact, I hardly know a strike is on. Bob never gets upset. Other than putting in a longer day, he's no different."

"You mean his work habits haven't changed because of the strike?"

"Only the extra time at the office, as I mentioned."

"He's not preoccupied when he gets home?"

"Never. He may get a phone call he wouldn't otherwise

get, but that's it. He's just his same happy ole self," she laughed.

On Saturday Bob gave me the whole day. I was visiting him to get the full details on his administrative system. The strike was still on but his mind was as far away from it as it could be.

"Oh, I never give it a thought. Why should I? We are using supervisory personnel and except for field work, installations, repairs, etc., we are absolutely up to date."

"How do you explain that?"

"The Four Basic Management Administrative Procedures—or, as we say, the 4BMAP System; my friend, it's as simple as that!"

"Tell me about it."

TWO

How to keep your division functioning during an emergency

The way to put a Procedural System under an acid test condition is to see if it works in an emergency. 4BMAP was getting such a test in Babbidge's division.

"During this strike, we won't miss a single administrative detail," Bob said as we got into a discussion on the nuts and bolts of management procedures. "Without it, we could be back-logged for months."

I asked him what administrative functions were being kept current.

"Every single one . . . billings, reports of all kinds, inventory controls, budgets, force size, indexes . . . everything. It's as current as it would be if we had a full complement."

"Hmm, you must have a lot of redundancy in your office," I challenged.

"Not at all. Remember, supervisory personnel from other departments such as engineering, traffic, commercial, etc., were pulled from their offices and are doing the office, assignment and test board work."

"Do you mean engineers, traffic managers, etc., are doing office work?"

"Exactly!"

"How are they trained so fast?"

"We don't train them. They simply take over a job station using the 4BMAP system to do it."

Amazing Efficiency

"Do you mean a manager who normally does engineering work is now doing, say, test board work, assignment work, etc.?"

"Well, we select people who have worked, perhaps ten or 15 years ago, with an ability to do testing, to handle jobs like those; but under the direction of an administrator supervisor and using the Job Procedures at the job station, they get the work done—accurately, and on time."

He talked about a field manager doing a complicated trouble analysis report.

"Never did one in his life. But he knew how to follow a Job Procedure because the details of filling out the report were there, step by step, and he could read—so the report was perfect."

Bob cited examples by the hour. With each one there was more attestation to the rather amazing efficiency of the 4BMAP system.

"O.K. Bob, let's get down to it," I was eagerly asking. "How did you come to develop the system?"

THREE

Setting up
a system that
frees you from
"traffic cop"
managing

The manager must stop being a traffic cop . . . must innovate . . . must be free to think and plan.

"I guess it was out of personal necessity," Bob replied. "When I was a first level manager I knew I had to have a system by which I could be certain I'd cover all bases . . . that I'd never be caught not having done something that needed to be done, or getting so tied up in knots over administrative detail that I would not be able to function as a manager—working *with* the men instead of just *for* them."

He said a manager is compensated primarily on his ability to think, plan, create and innovate. Most managers qualify but they become completely and literally consumed by detail work and haven't the time to discharge the function for which they are paid.

"They become traffic cops and their desks are busy intersections from which they route the flow of work. All day

long they unsnarl traffic jams, checking the speeders, pushing
the slows, ticketing the offenders. And, as with traffic cops,
they rarely get to know the drivers, where they came from or
where they are going!"

Bob faced that dilemma 20 years ago and made up his
mind it wasn't going to happen to him. As he rose in the
management ranks he kept expanding his administrative ideas.

An Administrative Discovery

"As a foreman I had three functions—keeping the work
current, the personnel happy, and myself programmed! That
was what produced the first phase of what has become known
as 4BMAP, or the Four Basic Management Administrative
Procedures, with, of course, the aid of outside expertise. The
first phase is known as 'the Planned Management Program and
Job Procedures.' We call them P.M.P.'s and J.P.'s.

"With a P.M.P. (Planned Management Program) I could
commit to a system every conceivable aspect of my administrative and supervisory function. It didn't require my memory. It all went into the system. That's why, even today, I
never have to think about my job function when I'm away
from it—unless of course I want to play around with a new
idea, and that's just plain fun!

"As for J.P.'s (Job Procedures), because I had men under
me I had to make sure they had a system that guaranteed
their continuous knowledge about how to do things. That's
what produced the J.P. phase, and right today you can go
into the field, ask a man how a certain job is done, and he
will show you a written, step-by-step description. If you
follow it even *you* could do most of the jobs they do—
except of course those jobs that require a high degree of craft
skill.

Overcoming Problems of Personnel Changes

"There was another thing I discovered back in those
days," he said, "the frequency of personnel changes. Men

were constantly being transferred, promoted, or terminated, and training replacements became a giant-sized time user. With Job Procedures, other than technical skills most of the training was eliminated."

He paused for a moment. "Here's an example. I get a kick out of the manager who loses his secretary and then looks for the hari-kari knife. You would think the world had come to an end. In the last 30 months I have had three new secretaries and when each one left, she did so because she was either promoted to a better supervisory position or placed in a position where she could get further experience and a possibility of future promotions."

Losing a secretary for Bob was as routine as losing a cuff link and not nearly as annoying. His training procedures for the new hire were simple and yet amazingly effective.

"When a replacement comes in I train her by allowing her to spend the first day reading the Job Procedures at her desk. I welcome her, then leave her alone.

"The next day, I keep an eye out to see how she is functioning, and about two weeks after she has been on the job I might bring her in, discuss some job detail, let her know she can adjust the steps on a function to suit her own methods—if they are better than those in the J.P.—and, well, she just does the job, that's it."

With a Planned Management Program to Use,
Even a Novice Could Take Over the Boss's
Administrative Tasks

Bob produced his own P.M.P. manual. It was a simple three-ring binder. Turned sideways it was a chronicle of management function done on a pre-printed form, and containing the action to be taken in every procedure from opening the office in the morning ("which is just for the edification of a successor") to filing employee evaluation reports, checking salary schedules, safety regulations, inventory levels, and the literally hundreds of functions a division manager must perform during the year.

The form had a wide column to describe the responsibility, another to describe the frequency of follow-up, a ruled-off section to permit the user to clearly mark the things done and not done, and a place for the month of the year in which the assignment is supposed to be done.

Scheduling Activities

"At the beginning of the month I flip through these pages. Because of my scheduling techniques it takes about half an hour to schedule my major activities for the entire month, which might include management meetings and agendas, other kinds of meetings, field visits for Detailed Job Inspections, visits of co-workers, etc."

He presented many illustrations as we flipped through his book.

In the "Description" column he covered such things as the name of the job function, the reference or authority for doing it, who does it, when it is done, where does it go, any special forms used, how it is handled when completed, and with many individual functions a brief description of why the job has to be done.

He handed me the book and asked me to glance at any page. I stopped flipping at a page and read the left-hand column. I read it aloud.

> I schedule a meeting with my immediate subordinates during November each year. The purpose is to evaluate all management people with potential to advance and those who are now ready for promotion. This is an all-day session and the arrangements for the meeting place, etc., are all handled by the division personnel supervisor.
>
> A) Schedule discussion of conference arrangements in my work group meeting during October.

Setting Up a Calendar

After I read it, Bob explained: "This is something I want to do every year. I do it in November and start arranging it in

October. Let's say we have just completed September and on the first of October I go through my P.M.P. pages. My eye is focused on the October section in the follow-up columns. I'm not interested in anything that is not to be done in October so I examine only that one column. Then I come across this oblique stroke in the October column. I look over to the description column and read what you just read. It tells me I have to put the conference in motion. It won't be held until November but I don't want to leave it till then. I want the place for it, the agenda, the location, etc., organized long before November. So this entry tells me to bring the subject of the conference to the October meeting. I then mark it down on my management meeting agenda form. When the meeting starts, it's right there. Having done that, I make another oblique stroke in the follow-up column which forms an X . . . indicating that item has been looked after. I don't give it another thought. It's on the agenda and I can forget about it.

"Other items that must be covered periodically at such meetings have all been typed in by the secretary in advance, for every month of the year, and this agenda preparation is noted on the P.M.P. so that I only have to have my secretary add current agenda items that come into my mind just prior to the meeting."

Having gone through one entry, I started examining others. Every entry representing a job responsibility already done had the X stroke in the follow-up column for the month. Obviously, as he completed the function, he completed the X. He said the completion stroke was as important as the initial listing and description of the particular assignment. This tells the manager what has to be done and whether it *is* done.

"Often a manager gets so busy he cannot even remember having done some things. This tells him. Or, if he gets so busy he forgets some job function this tells him the function wasn't done, because the second oblique stroke will not be recorded. This is great because occasionally there is an emergency and you might have to skip some items. But you skip them on purpose and you never forget them. They can be picked up later."

**If You Don't Know Accountability from
Responsibility, You Are in Deep Trouble . . . A
"Do-It-Yourselfer" Is Not a Competent Manager.
Delegate but Don't Abdicate!**

I was beginning to understand the real value of a P.M.P.
I looked at many pages. Every facet of his administrative,
personnel and technical responsibilities was recorded as to
just what he had to do. I became aware of the fact that he
had his job beautifully assigned to others. Each P.M.P. entry
outlined *what* he had to do but the *how* of it was usually
covered in an entry that read "See secretary's J.P." or "See
division manager's Operating Letter #112." I mentioned this
to Bob.

"There is a vast difference between job responsibility and
job accountability. As a manager you are *responsible* for
many things, but you should have others assume the accountable function!

Filing Work Force Reports

"For example, it's my responsibility to file work force
reports every month. It's a breakdown of our complement of
personnel. My secretary, however, is accountable for doing the
report, although she has one of her clerks actually doing the
labor. In order for me to know that she does it correctly, on
time, etc., I make sure she has a J.P. that spells out the
step-by-step processes in preparing the report . . . such as when
it must be prepared, what forms are used, where they are
located, how she writes it up, and so forth. And of course her
clerk has J.P.'s telling her what part she plays. This is
interesting because normally a secretary has all she can do to
keep the boss's work done, but by using J.P.'s she can also
perform quite a number of supervisory functions as well.

"I have a P.M.P. to remind me of my responsibility for
this report and she and some clerical person have J.P.'s to tell
them exactly *how* to prepare it."

Wage Costs Should Influence Delegation Decisions

He said too many managers fall into the trap of being
involved in the *accountable* function while trying to make
sure they are immune from oversights in the *responsible*
function.

"I know that report has to be done each month. It's
pretty important. Although I don't do reports of this nature I
have an accountability for them as well as a responsibility. So
I want to see they are done correctly.

"What happens with too many managers is this. They
know they have an accountability for this kind of report so
they often do it themselves. When you measure this as a cost
factor—the cost of their time against the cost of a clerk's
time—it becomes quite a needless expense and a fantastic
investment of time which could be used for many other
important assignments that require thinking and planning."

"Maybe," I said, "the work force report is easy to do
and your secretary and her clerk can do it. What about other
more difficult reports, or reports which are highly confiden-
tial, or ones which you know no one can do as well as you
can?"

"Believe it or not," he replied, "there are very few things
in a manager's administrative function that he cannot delegate
to a junior manager or a secretary. Managers *think* they have
to do a zillion things that others can do as well or better.
They become 'do-it-yourselfers' and they not only kill themselves with detail work, they also kill the incentive and
interest of their employees. They think they are good,
hard-working managers. Well, they are anything but."

How Abdication Can Perpetuate "Job Training"

"In other words, you believe in complete delegation," I
said.

"I certainly do, but there is quite a difference between
delegation and abdication. Many managers think they delegate

the accountable function . . . I mean, they let the secretary do the job, or someone else . . . but in actual fact they don't delegate, they *abdicate*.

"Let's stay with the work force report. I'm responsible for it. Suppose I teach my secretary how to do it and she learns fast. It goes into her head and she keeps it there. The reports come in month after month. I feel secure so I forget about the report. I don't even know how it's produced anymore. I just sign it as it is laid on my desk.

"Now this could happen with many reports. Let's say I've got a good secretary, so I keep handing the accountable functions to her. I'm proud of myself. It's real delegation," he said sarcastically.

"Well, it isn't. It is real abdication. I abdicate not only the accountable function, I abdicate the responsible function as well.

"Then one day Miss Jones comes in. 'I'm getting married next month and will be leaving the company, Mr. Babbidge!' And I reach for the gas hose. I'm done. I have to train a girl all over again. But that's not so difficult. What's difficult is this—I have to train *myself* all over again. Over a year or two, unless I spend every waking hour remembering the job detail, it will disappear from memory. Since I've abdicated the detail and the responsibility for two years, you can be sure it will be virtually gone from my mind, and I have no alternative but to start from scratch."

How to Delegate

"O.K.," I said, "how can you delegate completely without losing the memory of the detail?"

"Through Job Procedures. The secretary or someone else wrote the J.P. and when it was completed it was either checked by someone with knowledge of the function or by myself, to make sure it was done accurately. So the complete detail on how the report is produced, when, what forms, etc., is on a page in the secretary's J.P. I don't *have* to remember the detail. It's all there. When a new secretary comes in she takes over the J.P.'s at her desk, and as I've said, she studies them, and is capable of doing the report accurately the first time. I don't have to teach her, and what's more important, I don't have to teach myself!"

The Blackmailed Boss Is a Cinch to Crack
Under the Strain; with J.P.'s Everyone
Can Be Replaced

"I'm beginning to see what you mean," I said. "In fact, I can see another trap a manager can fall into. It's just a bit different than the 'do-it-yourselfer' trap. It's the manager who delegates the accountable function but stretches his memory every day by holding the fine details in his mind."

"Correct," he smiled. "You're learning, all right. There are hundreds of managers who do this. They're afraid of being blackmailed by the so-called indispensable employee ... the one who holds you up for a raise because he knows you will be in grief if he leaves. And to protect yourself you memorize his accountable function so that you can always accept his resignation and always be ready to teach someone else. If you have 20 employees it becomes quite a memory feat. I don't know of anyone who can do it, but they probably try. Can you imagine how their minds get tied in knots?"

"I sure can," I agreed, "but isn't there something else involved here for the busy, busy manager ... the one who has dozens of responsible functions ... like your job, for instance? As I look through this P.M.P. of yours I would guess there are probably a hundred or so pages in it. Each one describes one or two of your responsibilities. Is this why you can forget your own job when you leave it?"

"Of course!" he exclaimed. "I don't have to remember anything. It's in the system. All I have to do is follow the system and everything I need to do to fill this job is automatically going to come to my attention when it needs to be done. Of course I may be missing something but when I find out about it, I add it to the P.M.P.—which means I tag one more base.

The Critical Test of a System Comes When a Subordinate Takes Over Your Job Station

"Do you want to take over your boss's job? You can, you know," he said as he pushed the book at me. Bob asked me to make two assumptions.

"First, assume that your district managers will give you their 100% cooperation. Second, you will never have to carry out a craft function . . . one that would require a trades skill. Now with those two assumptions, you tell me if you couldn't do my job right now; perhaps a little slower, but nothing would get by you. You might even do it better than I'm doing it after awhile because you could bring your expertise to the job and that, added to my own, could easily combine to make a much better result from this office."

I was dumbfounded at the suggestion. Run a division with hundreds of people in it . . . and tag all the bases right now! Ridiculous! Or was it? As I studied the pages, read the descriptions of each responsibility, realized that the detail was not only done by others but they had written procedures for doing it (which I could study at any time), I slowly began to understand how I might be able to make it!

"There isn't a doubt about it," he affirmed. "You have leadership ability. You're a good administrator—you know how to deal with people—so with P.M.P.'s like these you couldn't miss, and remember this—with these P.M.P.'s you have all the routine and all of the experience I have been able to bring to the job. You can literally claim it was your own because it is all set down in writing and in step-by-step detail. You would only have to follow the system and you wouldn't miss a single thing. Now in time you would introduce your own expertise to the job and, as I said, wind up doing a better job than I'm doing."

FOUR

How to
vastly increase
your
discretionary
time

Bob is almost a fanatic on the subject of "discretionary time" availability. He maintained that a manager who had any at all was the exception.

"What is your definition of discretionary time?" I asked.

"That is the time a manager has available in each working day to think and plan. As I said, that's what the guy is really paid for . . . to think and plan . . . to innovate after he creates. To the degree he doesn't do this, he's not a manager at all. He's a traffic cop or a highly paid clerk, but certainly not a manager."

"Well, today's manager is just too busy to have that kind of free time," I said. "His time is simply consumed by his responsibilities and, as you say, his accountabilities."

"Not true," he retorted. "Let me give you some ideas on picking up hours every day. In fact, with many so-called managers I can show you changes that can be made that would literally eliminate their position. This would be particularly significant in government offices, school systems, hospitals and, of course, a few large companies!"

How to Stop the New Hire from
Devouring Your Time

Bob talked about training and detail supervision time.

"Most managers are held responsible for training and supervising their people. It begins when an employee arrives at the job station. The manager goes through an induction interview, introduces the employee to his or her associates, and then begins the instruction on each and every assignment. This presumes of course that he knows every intricate detail of the assignments the new employee will take over—and you would be surprised how many employees are hired without anyone knowing or thinking about any details of the engagement. More than that, I'd like to see a manager who would know every intricate detail of a subordinate's job. It's impossible!

"His time is now at the disposal of the new employee. In order to get him productive the manager devotes the first hours to the most important assignment the employee will have. And that might take hours, the first time around. But the job is done. So back to the desk goes the manager.

"How long do you think it will be before the employee comes to him with a question? Not very long, or if he doesn't come to the manager, he will go to a co-worker. The co-worker may not know the answer but he will try to *offer* an answer. After ten to 20 minutes he will wind up saying, 'Oh, I really don't know. Better ask so and so.'

"Well, so and so may have a general idea but it's mighty unlikely to be exactly the method the boss wants to produce the result he expects. If the job is *then* done after this incorrect direction, the boss will have to take some more time to explain *again* exactly how *he* wants it done, or it may be necessary for him to look it up in a company manual which he hasn't checked for months and then take hours to read it, understand it, and explain it to the new employee.

Counting Up the Time Involved

"Now count the time involved. First, direct person-to-person training time. Second, co-worker discussions. Third, more boss/employee training time or manual research and explaining time. Until that employee gets that assignment *down to memory,* this training and supervising time might go on for months. And of course, this assumes he can remember every detail during these months—and nobody can—so mistakes are made all through these months and more time is lost.

"With every segment of the employee's job function handled this way you can be sure that the boss or a co-worker and the employee are going to lose hours and hours constantly."

"But isn't that one of those inevitable problems for any manager?" I asked.

"The training and supervising part is, but it's *how* it's done that counts!" replied Bob. "If that job function was clearly spelled out in a Job Procedure, the employee would first study it—by himself—and with the step-by-step procedures laid out, could do the job without asking any questions at all. The boss's training time is practically eliminated.

"By following the procedures the employee learns by doing. He simply does each step in sequence as he follows a Job Procedure. It takes no longer to orient the employee in the first place, and because he has written instructions to follow he will ask fewer questions, and will be doing it right in most cases, immediately."

In-Office "Baby Sitting" Can Be Stopped

"Well, don't most companies assign a new girl to another employee and let her get her training by working with the employee?" I asked.

"They sure do—and by doing so they guarantee the loss of the productive time of both employees. It doesn't matter whether it is an employee or a manager who does the training. Whoever does it is going to lose a lot of productive time. The new hire becomes little more than a helper and she or he may be a helper for months. The employee doing the training is effectively a baby sitter, and the employee who is being 'sat' is contributing nothing."

"I'm beginning to see what you mean," I nodded. "Under your system the new employee actually gets most of his training by studying and following Job Procedures, then actually doing the job. It could save both the boss and the employee time, but would it really be a significant amount of time?"

"It sure would be significant with most managers, and the reason is simple. Take employee changes—transfers, promotions, resignations, etc. Every time the training phase is done, everyone, including the boss, loses time. Add it up over a year and it represents a fantastic amount of lost productive time, and just a tremendous baby-sitting fee!

How to Set Priorities—Handle a Crisis—and Have Time Left Over

"Another source of discretionary time for the manager is the elimination of the daily memory exercise he goes through," Bob said.

"Do you mean remembering his priorities?" I asked.

"Yes, that and other types of exercises. Priority assessment is bad enough. Some managers have been on the job for years and still have to think about priorities. The reason is simply confusion, and they are kept confused about the priorities because they have no system for analyzing them, for getting them in front of them *before the month begins.*"

"But aren't priorities often upset? Doesn't it often happen that you go to work intending to do something and something else becomes more important?" I asked.

"That's exactly right," Bob agreed. "However, because one

priority replaces another the manager is still conscious of not having done the first one. So, he bobbles that in his mind while he takes on the new priority. Often that one gets preempted for still a third one, so he now bobbles two. Then he may be involved in the kind of a job where he seems to be going from crisis to crisis. Now the manager might bobble a half a dozen priorities.

Reorganizing Priorities

"This is when things get really confusing and this is when a whale of a lot of time is lost in simply reorganizing the priorities. I mean *real* time. The guy can lose 15 minutes every hour just thinking about the job priorities and planning his moves so as to try to cover them all. That type is ulcer prone! He has so many balls in the air he can't juggle them all and then he starts burying work, not doing it at all, hiding his oversights, rushing his assignments, fretting his memory. Wow! This guy can become a real mess."

"O.K.," I said eagerly, remembering how I fitted the description many times in the past, "how does he bobble priorities, face crisis after crisis, and *not* go out of his tree and *not* waste a lot of time?"

"All right!" he said, "let's go back to the P.M.P. Look at mine.

"Let's say it's August first. I go through the pages and through scheduling techniques I pick off all the things I have to do this month. These items wind up on a planning calendar. I take care that I spread the work over the entire month so I don't wind up on the 15th or the 25th or any other day, doing more than I want to do on that day. Now there's my month's work laid out for me. I know what I have to do on each working day. O.K. Let's take Wednesday, the 20th of August. On that day my planning calendar says I have to visit the division emergency center to check records, discuss communications, etc. That can take the best part of a morning. In the afternoon I can take care of the normal routine of the job such as assigning and reviewing reports, answering calls and doing some planning.

A Change in the Plan

"That's my whole day's work. Now I come in that morning and the first thing that greets me is a message from one of the district managers telling me they had a fire in the plant the night before. When that happens, a lot of things must be done at once! Reports galore have to be made up. I have to personally inspect the premises. Losses have to be established. Management and other departments have to be called. Oh, there are a lot of things involved. So there goes my day's work. My priorities have been completely upset."

"So you leave the office to check up on the fire," I said. "How does this eliminate time loss in respect to your other priorities?"

"In two ways. First, I don't worry about the ones I'm *not* doing. They are on my planning calendar and because they aren't done they are going to stay there until they are done. I know I'm going to be tied up with that fire for the whole day. In about one minute I tell my secretary to rearrange appointments, etc. If any reports are to come in for my signature I tell her to give them to one of my subordinates who can check my P.M.P. and find out exactly what to do with the reports."

Returning to Routine

"Well, this hasn't saved you any time," I said.

"It hasn't, eh? Well, you just think about what happens when the crisis is over and I have to get my brains in gear trying to remember what it was I was supposed to be doing instead of attending to the fire details."

"Well, you do have a scheduling system. You can check back quite easily," I said.

"I sure do, and isn't that just what we've been talking about? I *know* what hasn't been done. I don't have to *think* about it or *remember* it. There it sits on the calendar or one of the other scheduling forms. These are part of the system . . . and it's the system that's missing with so many managers."

"Sorry, Bob," I said, "but that sounds pretty basic. If a man doesn't use a planning calendar he probably uses something else. Or, wouldn't he just plain remember what he had to do?"

"Yes, it's possible. Not probable . . . but possible. The significant point is, he doesn't *have* to remember. The system does that for him."

I was trying to relate what he was saying to my own experience in the past. I didn't work with a well-developed system. As I thought about it, it began to dawn on me that when my priorities were upset I *did* go through memory exercises. I could distinctly remember having to admit to someone that because of such and such an event I simply forgot to do something I was supposed to do or had promised to do.

I wanted to explore it further. "I think the illustration you gave—the plant fire—was too cut and dried. You obviously had your whole day rearranged so you simply moved the things on the calendar for that day over to another day. Right?"

"That's right. And if the fire took up my time for more than a day I would be moving things to be done to subsequent days."

"But this just defers." I said, "It doesn't solve . . . nor does it reduce your time investment. Undoubtedly you wind up trying to do three days' work in one!"

Knowing Precisely What Has to Be Done

"True, but I know precisely *what hasn't been done.* I may have to put in a little extra time to catch up, but the thing to remember is that *nothing* goes unattended. And that brings me to the second way time is saved. It's not my time. It's other people's time. Because other managers have P.M.P.'s and non-managers have J.P.'s, the jobs can continue to be done. The man who heads up my work force can take over my P.M.P. and literally do the job. All he needs to know is how . . . and the P.M.P. tells him.

"Managers who do not work with this system find, when an emergency is over, they have much of their own work not done, but they also find that in many ways they have become a bottleneck for many of their managers and sub-managers and their subordinates. By the time these bottlenecks are cleared everyone will have invested hours of time in a 'catching up' program."

Gradually it was becoming clear to me that without the system some things could literally get out of control. Job responsibilities could be forgotten, people left waiting, reports not completed or filed, which trigger their own ripple of lost time for those involved.

A Matter of Control

"Of course I can accept the fact that a fair amount of time *is* lost when you lose sight of uncompleted priorities," I said, "but isn't the most important aspect of the P.M.P. phase and its planning calendar component a matter of control more than time saving?"

"Well, I won't withdraw my statement on the time factor because if you think about it enough you will agree that a lot of time *is* lost in just trying to remember what wasn't done. With this system you *know* what isn't done and you pick up the job exactly where you left it. Other members of the work group do not lose a lot of time with backlogs created by the manager's forgetfulness. But you are right when you speak of control. Being able to make an accurate decision on what you *won't* do is about as important as being able to decide what you *will* do.

"Few managers have the choice. They just plow through a work load without consideration of real priorities. They lurch from one detail to another and as a rule they start interfering with their own priorities."

"What do you mean by that?" I asked.

"Don't you ever start something knowing it has to be done

and suddenly remember there is something more important for you to be doing? You stop what you are doing, lurch into the other function, and if that happens two or three times, the first thing you find is that the job you started never gets done at all. So what you are actually doing is interfering with your own priorities. It's bad enough having other people or other events interfere with them, but when you start doing it yourself, you're in trouble."

How to Analyze a Job into Component Parts and Get the *Whole* Picture

I agreed that I had done this many times but I felt at the time I had no alternative. What I wanted to know was whether the system could eliminate what I considered to be simple normal confusion at almost any job station. I couldn't remember a time in my past management history when I had any day-to-day control, but somehow I thought I got the job done. Although as I was now thinking about it, I probably missed plenty. As I reflected on some of those positions I admitted to myself I didn't have any real appreciation of having priorities. Everything seemed to be a priority. I just had a job to do and I did it as expeditiously as I could.

"Bob, I've been thinking about my own past history," I said. "I've had jobs which seemed to be just one big priority. They were like a continuous function. I began it at the beginning of the month and kept doing it until the end of the month. I know I did many different things but when I take an objective look at it, it would have been hard for me to detail, as a special job function, any one of the specific parts of the job."

Looking at the Parts

"And you are typical of most managers," he explained. "You look at the total job instead of the component parts of it. If you took a piece of paper and thought about it for a few minutes, you would find that your total responsibility breaks down into clearly defined job functions. For instance, I'll bet you had work force management responsibilities, employee evaluation reports, salary reports, holiday schedules and so forth. You probably had certain housekeeping responsibilities. Perhaps you were involved in quality measuring programs, work group meetings, overtime controls, government reports, purchasing, customer services, stationery controls, client relationships, advertising. Oh, the list could be as long as your arm. But you'd go from one function to another without even realizing that your job is made up of a dozen or more components . . . some of which you attend to religiously, some you do when you think about it, some you forget to do entirely, and get a first class shock when some auditor or inspector points it out to you.

"In effect, what is supposed to be an organized job function is really little more than a big chunk of marble. You keep chipping away at it hoping that one day it will shape up into some recognizable form or statue. But it never does. It just stays as a chunk of hard stone . . . a clump of responsibility. You can't even *visualize* it as a smooth statue, never mind knock it into the shape of one!"

"You're coming through now," I said.

"I sure hope so," he smiled. "This is the very thing that kills effective management. Without getting a model of that statue on paper, how can you ever knock it into shape? You chip a bit here and a bit there and you still have nothing but a big rock . . . unless of course, you are a sculptor . . . and even then the statue will be clearly outlined in your *mind* before you pick up the chisel."

Chipping Away at Responsibilities

I had no difficulty realizing how accurate he was. That's exactly what I used to do in the past. Chip away at each of my responsibilities but rarely see or even visualize the whole position . . . or statue. The analogy was perfect. If the job function had been broken down I then could have seen what I was doing, where it would lead me, who would be doing it, when, how and why. In other words, the picture of the statue would be complete in my mind, because it was complete on paper.

"That's quite an accurate analogy, Bob," I said. "I can see now why there is that general feeling of confusion or lack of purpose with so many management positions. The incumbent hasn't drawn a picture of the statue he's trying to hack out!"

"Right on the button," he laughed. "The poor man is banging the chisel all day but he never gets any real shape resulting. The job function is just like the rock. When you do it without a planned program you make a helluva pile of rock chips but you never get a Venus de Milo. And when you upset your priorities you forget where you hit the rock last. As a result it just gets more out of shape!"

How to Eliminate 90% of Your Accountabilities

Bob took a piece of paper, drew a line down the middle and handed it to me. "Now, in the left column you list all of your different job functions...job responsibilities. On the right and opposite each listing, just write the name of the person who is accountable for that responsibility."

I went to work. In ten minutes I had 14 different responsibilities listed. I held myself accountable for ten of them and my secretary for four. Bob examined it carefully. "And you are the one who said your position was just one big priority. I can see 14 right here. But that's not too important. Why are you holding *yourself* accountable for so many? For instance, you have to file a sales tax return to the government. Do you prepare that report?"

"Well, I prepare most of it. It has to be accurate."

"Is your secretary not as accurate as you are?"

"I suppose she is."

"Did you ever set up a Job Procedure for her on how to do the report?"

"No."

"Then why don't you?"

"Never thought of it . . . never met you in time," I laughed.

"How much time does it take to do it?"

"Only about an hour every month."

"You've just saved yourself an hour a month!"

We eagerly went down the entire list. When we were through I had four accountable functions and the secretary had the other ten. I admitted that with Job Procedures written out, the secretary would have no difficulty doing the jobs as I wanted them done. In time saved, I was looking at 11 hours, and I hadn't even started to break my job function down.

"Now that is just a small example of what happens when a manager takes the first step in the Planned Management Program. He starts to see his job objectively instead of subjectively. He's above it instead of being buried in it. He's in control of it instead of being controlled by it. With it *planned out* and *programmed* into the system, he can juggle his priorities, have them interfered with by the crises and still not miss a step. Moreover, when he sorts out his accountabilities from his responsibilities, he winds up with hours of discretionary time availability. I've seen discretionary time expand so much that it eliminates the position."

How to Change an "Empire Builder" into a Proficient Manager

"Kind of tough on the guy eliminated," I said.

"You *don't* eliminate the man. You could promote him to bigger and better things or move him laterally into a job where a manager is required. If you hired him to be a manager and he acted like a manager by getting his job under such perfect control, why wouldn't you promote him? *He's* the guy you *need* in a company. He's the guy who will spot the empire builders and expose them for what they are. But even that isn't right. The empire builder is usually a guy who has lost control of his job function and hires people and keeps hiring people to cover up his loss of control. If he were guided into Planned Management Programming he would reduce his work force accordingly. The empire builder is simply short on management systems. He's frightened. He hires people to protect *his* job. Give him the system and he'll straighten out the over-staff position every time. Why? Because he's no longer afraid or confused. He controls the job instead of it controlling him. The 4BMAP system does *not* eliminate people by lay-offs or dismissals. Work force redundancy looks after itself when it is exposed. People are always leaving a company. You just don't replace them when you don't need them."

"It sounds like a pretty thin line difference, Bob," I said. "If a job is eliminated by a system, don't you think senior management is going to lay off the person involved?"

"If there is no place in the organization for him they will lay him off. They have no alternative. But a *growing* company isn't in that position too often. What they have done is opened the way for a substantial increase in productivity without having to engage another employee to accomplish it. And that's the position management should be taking. The 4BMAP system is not a retrenching system; it's an expansion system that permits larger volumes without larger costs."

Dealing with Redundancy

"When its installation is discussed with management, would the possibility of the system exposing some redundancy be pointed out?" I asked.

"By all means. It happens every time the system is installed. There *is* redundancy in the vast majority of offices, and 4BMAP will expose it. But instead of saying to a client that he can lay off a half-dozen people, they suggest to him that he can enjoy a substantial improvement in productivity, and not have to engage a single person."

"In spite of your observation," I insisted, "I'm sure that if redundancy is exposed, people are going to be laid off."

"That's up to the management, of course. If it has

overloaded its work force in comparison to its volume, it had better lay them off or go broke. But I still say, on the experience of consultants who are making installations of the 4BMAP system they are seeing expanded production, and in place of lay-offs they are seeing a policy of attrition being introduced."

"In other words, if they quit, you don't rehire, right?"

"Right!"

FIVE

How to make
a system do
what you force
your memory to do-and
do it better

"Did you ever see a manager re-invent the wheel every time he needs one?" Bob asked laughingly.

"I don't understand."

"A manager has just completed one assignment and is about to start another. The vast majority of them now go through a little mental gymnastics. It takes the form of sub-vocalized questions. Here are a few of them.

" 'What do I do next?' Priorities again. Then, 'Let's see now, how do I do this?' 'Who does that part of it?' 'When is it supposed to be done?' 'Just what is the deadline?' 'Where do I get the information?' 'Who signs it?' 'How will I be judged on it?'

"These gymnastics take place with each assignment and the more infrequently the assignment is done, the more gymnastic time is invested. Things that have to be done quarterly can take 40 minutes of gymnastics. The amount of time becomes less and less through frequency. Daily assignments require practically no exercises.

"But if you add these gymnastic periods together, they can add up to many, many hours– and the manager's time is literally devoted to 're-inventing the wheel.' "

"That might apply to the relatively new manager, but surely it does not apply to the experienced one," I said.

"Believe me, the experienced manager today is a rare bird! Through growth a good man is not likely to have the same job more than three years, and that's not much experience. But let's assume he has had the job for ten years. Is it the same job? Perhaps it has the same title, but you can be certain that except in a very small group of companies or departments in large companies, the incidence of change has reorganized or reclassified the job functions and the procedures for carrying them out.

Changing Managerial Functions

"Permanent job titles rarely equate to permanent job functions. Responsibilities under a job title tend to expand; procedures and systems are almost always in a state of change; company policies and objectives change; work force is changing regularly, government regulations, union demands and management desires keep the pot boiling all the time.

"Often, the mental gymnastics I mentioned are necessary simply to assure the manager he is doing things the *new* way, not the old way! And that's where the so-called experienced manager can be in trouble. His ways tend to become fixed, stereotyped, while he is involved in anything but a fixed or stereotyped environment. It's like stepping off to the inside of a moving merry-go-round. Things are dead still on the inside but to get back to where the public is, the victim has a lot of fast footwork ahead of him.

"If he can do it at all it's because he performs those mental gymnastics. And that, without a system, is where the time is lost, and things get fouled up or are missed completely.

"And incidentally," he added, "that is where the rise to

your level of incompetence can be seen. Regrettably, the *system* is usually more incompetent than the *man*. But *it* isn't judged . . . the man is! And he's judged as incompetent."

"So it boils down to the man trying to remember the system," I said, "instead of the system acting as the memory bank for the man?"

"Precisely! But, he *has* to remember the system if one is not written down for him so the time he takes in doing that is essentially wasted every time he tackles an assignment."

"But Bob, isn't a good memory just one more qualification that separates the manager from the non-manager?"

"Yes, to a degree. But I think it's like saying that good penmanship eliminates the need for a typewriter, or mathematical competence does away with the adding machine.

"For centuries we have heard about the mind's phenomenal capacity to store and retain bits of information. I think one writer said we could easily handle ten billion bits of information, but in a normal life span we are lucky if we can handle a fraction of a percentage of the ten billion bits.

"Others say we use only 10% or 20% of our capacity . . . and others say the capacity is infinite . . . so what's 20% of infinity?

"The point is, we know all this . . . or have been told these things all our lives . . . but we still have millions of people who can't remember where they put their umbrella or their pen, or the procedures they follow to do a quarterly report.

Finding a Memory Substitute

"I think it's time to face up to a few unalterable facts. We have a few memory freaks in this world, but they aren't in offices. They are on stages frustrating their audiences who think *they* should be able to do the same thing. I wonder why they don't feel the same frustration when they watch a fire eater or a sword swallower? I imagine it's because they don't eat fire or swords on the job. But on the job they are judged on their *memory,* and it sends them wild when they forget.

"More important from the company's standpoint is what a poor memory or an average memory can mean when a detail or a priority at a job station is forgotten. The result of either can be serious and costly. But what are we doing? Insisting that the memory be *trusted*! Judging the man on his *memory ability,* likely promoting him on his memory ability!"

"Well, is that bad?" I asked.

"As I said before, not any worse than using penmanship instead of typing a letter, or counting beads instead of using an adding machine. Don't get me wrong, there's nothing wrong with a good hand or the ability to count beads, but in this day they are outdated talents!"

"Are you suggesting that we have moved so close to total automation that a man doesn't have to use his memory?" I queried.

"Not at all, and it will never get to that stage. I'm suggesting that typing a letter, or using an adding machine, is the easier and faster way of doing things. And, the time that is saved can be used more advantageously."

"So the 4BMAP system is a timesaver more than a crutch to a weak memory?" I suggested.

"I suppose it's both. Certainly, it's a timesaver and a means to dramatically improve accuracy. As for the crutch, it's probably that too. You'll have to admit that with a crutch the one-legged man can at least walk!"

"So you think the average man's mind is—like—one-legged?" I smiled.

"That may be too brutal. What I'm saying is that management responsibility has become very complex. Obviously, from the mistakes made in industry, too complex, and I think industry should face up to it. There are many people in the world who believe you can 'think' disease out of the system, but lots of them die with cancer.

"If top-level management continues to believe that all sub-management and non-management job detail is going to be *remembered,* they are just doing the same things as the 'thinkers' do with disease, the handwriter does with a type-writer, and the bead expert does with an adding machine.

"They are either kidding themselves or they like to die, write or count. Similarly, if you and I—or any manager—think we can remember all of our job detail instantly and accurately, we are kidding *ourselves.*"

"So, your point is," I interjected, "regardless of what they say about our memory capacity, it just ain't so, right?"

Making Room for Creative Work

"It just ain't so," he laughed. "And if it were so, you can be sure the manager has very little room left in his think-tank to do any creative work. I don't care what the capacity is, I only care about what we have experienced . . . and our experience shows that the memory of job detail requires continuous mental research which is clearly revealed at job stations all over the world by the mental gymnastics you see managers going through every time they take on a different assignment within their total job responsibility."

"Even though they may do those assignments accurately," I countered.

"Of course. They must be doing them fairly accurately or they wouldn't have the job. In all probability, however, if their total job was to be audited by a company auditor, the chances are a hundred to one they are overlooking many job details that should be done. But it's the time it takes them to get organized mentally in order to *do* them accurately that bothers me. It's the needless strain on their memory banks that denies them the capacity for a creative approach and it's the needless stress they experience as they try to keep track of the detail. Here's where the ulcers, coronaries, breakdowns come from, and here's where their rise to their incompetence levels is so frequently revealed."

"Let me get that straight," I said. "You're saying that because managers try to commit the detail of their job assignments to memory instead of to a system, they are overloading their think-tanks? They tie themselves into mental knots trying to keep step-by-step procedures for discharging their job responsibilities in their heads. Is that right?"

"Precisely!"

"Well, by what criteria do you judge a manager? Surely the guy should have a clear memory of the detail of his job function. If he hasn't got that, has he got *anything*?"

"It's trying to *maintain* a clear memory of the detail that makes him less effective than he could be. The criteria for judging a manager are no longer valid if they center on his ability to remember detail. If his thought process is consumed by that exercise, he will be found to be missing in the areas of creativeness, innovations, progressive thinking and so forth. In effect, he functions as a human memory bank inside of a computer . . . and I've never met a computer yet that ever sparked an original idea!"

"But he *must* remember the procedural steps involved in discharging his job function," I insisted.

"Why should he?"

"How else will things get done? If he doesn't remember the steps to take to do an assignment, the assignment isn't going to get done."

Handling Hundreds of Different Assignments

"Why should he *remember* them? Why not let a *system* remember them and leave his memory capacity, which takes up much of his *thinking* capacity, free for important work? I have hundreds of different assignments to perform. Each one is handled with different procedures. If I committed all those procedures to memory I wouldn't be doing anything else but keeping them straight in my mind. But I *should* say this . . . because they are *in* this sytem and because I make frequent reference *to* the system, I *do* remember a great deal more than I really need to remember. It's like a conditioned memory with exposures to the written word being the conditioning agent."

"But the experts say you *have* the ability to remember

without conditioning and *still* have room for a whole lot more," I said.

"I know what the experts say, but I'm talking about actual experience. The memory freak is, as I said, on the stage. Let him stay there. I'm interested in the man . . . or the manager . . . on the street. He's *not* a memory freak. He's a human being with all the limitations of a human being . . . and a human being in business has, whether we like to admit it or not, a definite limit to what he can safely remember by way of job procedures."

"So we've been judging a man wrong when we judge him primarily on his memory ability?" I asked.

"Of course we have. When men and women couldn't produce enough statistics . . . due to human limitations . . . for management to get accurate pictures to work with, what did management do? They installed computers. Did this in any way affect the reputation of those who couldn't produce the statistics?"

"No, I don't think it did," I responded. "It just eliminated their jobs."

Using People in More Productive Ways

"There's too much evidence to the contrary. Computers are blamed for cutting off job opportunities. Have you ever studied a company that installed computers? If you have you will see very little job displacement. In fact, the opposite is true. And the reason is simple. The people whose function was taken over by a computer were used in more productive ways. Their talents were not lost, just directed into a different job function. With the aid of the computer, management made more accurate decisions. It made them faster. It permitted expansion all the way down the line. Why? Because some of the guesswork was removed from the decision-making process. The companies grew. Although I must say that people who handle computers are the source of a lot of computer-blamed headaches. Here again, the human memory limitation. If the programmer forgets, so does the computer. But as for lay-offs, don't blame the computer. When Henry Ford introduced the assembly line concept, a lot of people said then that Ford would lay off hundreds of workers. Did that happen? Check the figures. The company increased its payroll a few thousand times!

"And it's exactly the same when we install a system that makes it unnecessary for a man to remember every facet of his job procedures. It's foolish to burden the mind that way. On a major management position it can drive the man crazy. He gets to the point where he is afraid to shake his head in case something drops out. He can become totally preoccupied with his job function. At home he is in trouble. The kids think he's angry at them and his wife thinks he's ignoring her. There he sits, lost in thought about what he has to do tomorrow, what he didn't do today, what he forgot to do yesterday. What a helluva way to live!"

"I must admit, Bob," I said, "you're a pretty good example of what you are saying. You just don't seem to be occupied with your job responsibilities at all. I've never met a man who was so relaxed, and who had a job the dimension of yours."

"Thank you. I enjoy my job and it's not that big. There are many in the system a whale of a lot bigger. But I wouldn't be any different if I had one of them. I don't fight my limitations. I just build systems under them. I don't want my home time to be interfered with by my job . . . so I have a system that makes that unnecessary."

How Job Details Are Remembered

"Don't you keep any job detail in your mind?"

"Very little, although the system, because I'm into it repeatedly, automatically conditions detail into the memory. But I'll tell you how far it goes." (He paused to contemplate his illustration.) "We have some pretty stiff security regulations. Most of the desks and filing cabinets are kept locked. If I wanted to get the key for my secretary's desk I could look it up in my P.M.P. and find out where it's located. Here, I'll show you."

He looked up the index at the front of the binder and found the section called "SECURITY." He got the page number, flipped over to the page and started looking down the description column. He read it aloud:

Office Keys:

The key to my secretary's desk is kept in my top desk drawer. Unlock secretary's desk and you find a small 3 X 5 card system. The system has keys on each card and describes the cabinets, desks and offices the keys will unlock. After using keys be sure to put them back in the same sequence in which you obtained them.

"That's a very simple illustration, and actually I wouldn't need to do it because I remember the routine."

"Then why have it written in your P.M.P.?" I asked. "You remember it!"

"I remember it because it is simple to do. It's no strain at all and I keep it in my P.M.P. for a very special reason. What happens if you take over my job? I'd have to explain it all to you. As it is, you can go right to it. I don't need to mention it to you."

I lost *that* round!

How to Remember Procedure Details Forever

"Let me give you another example," he said. "I'm responsible for an inventory report every month. There are definite procedures in developing it. You have to make up reports on losses, thefts or usage. It involves a fair amount of digging. Now, so help me, I wouldn't at this moment even try to tell you how it's done, even though I've been doing it for years. But I'll tell you how fast I can get the whole routine into my mind. Over to my P.M.P. again, I just look down the index page until I come to "INVENTORY." Here it is . . . Page 97. I flip it to page 97 and what does it say?

Inventory:

A. I'm responsible for the division's inventory report. It is made up and I sign it every month on the 25th.
B. A sample of the report is attached.
C. My secretary obtains district inventory reports by the 23rd of each month. She consolidates the figures and posts them to the division inventory report.
D. Details for gathering the information are contained in the secretary's J.P. and are also covered in Operating Letter #160.
E. When the secretary brings me the report I study it, and if O.K. I sign. If changes are necessary I notify my secretary and she makes the changes.

"Now if I wanted to refresh my memory on the gathering procedures I could look it up in my secretary's Job Procedures, or read Operating Letter #160 which was prepared by one of my work group and which laid out the detail I wanted followed within this division.

How P.M.P. Provides Freedom

"So," he continued, "with your P.M.P. you have a reminder that the report has to be done, a column to stroke off when it is done, and a brief outline of what you do and what others do in getting the report ready. And that's the way it is with virtually every function I have. Because of seeing the P.M.P. item quite frequently I may remember quite a bit of it. But I don't *have* to, and of course with the hundreds of individual responsibilities I have there are many I cannot recall in *any* detail, but I can sit and talk to you all day without them passing through my mind once . . . even when there's a strike on!"

"And yet, because of your P.M.P. binder, you won't miss a single trick," I said.

"Not one, and as new tricks, as you say, come up, they just go into the P.M.P. and I forget them."

"That's real freedom, Bob. Fantastic! What I most like about it is the realization that you are setting a whole new dimension to management effectiveness. You are freeing us poor guys who have believed all our lives that we have to memorize job details or procedures . . . that we are judged on our memory ability and that our raises depend on it! Here you are with a system that in effect eliminates memory as a major component in the make-up of a really good administrator. It's quite wonderful! In fact, as I think about some administrators whom I know personally, it could be a lifesaver for them."

"Well, that may be a little strong!" he continued, "But it can sure cut down the ulcers and make the average home a lot happier. That preoccupied husband is getting to be a fairly familiar figure in living rooms across this country."

"And in divorce courts," I added.

"How true," said Bob as he poured another cup of coffee. "I know a few who took that route. Damn shame! Nice couples. Good husbands. Good providers, but totally immersed in their job function. I mean *totally* immersed." He put his cup down and picked up his P.M.P. binder. "Do you think I could be as free from the job as I am right now if I had to carry all that detail in this book in my head? No way!"

Using Time Effectively

"It occurs to me, Bob, that it would take you a fair amount of time to get your job responsibilities outlined into a P.M.P. like that. How much time would a manager invest to get his job into the system?"

"Initially," he replied, "it will seem like a fair amount of *extra* time. That's only because we have no awareness of the time we now use up in mental gymnastics, poorly thought out procedures, mistakes, oversights, etc. If we gathered all that time together and measured it against the time it takes to program a manager's responsibilities, we would always be on the right side of the ledger. However, to answer that question—*yes,* it does require extra time. But it's time well invested for a manager. Instead of just putting in time he can now put something into time.

"Think about it," he emphasized. "Here's a multi-faceted administrative job. The incumbent is bending under the load. Probably his hands are so full some of his responsibilities are slipping through his fingers. He hasn't a minute to spare. He's taking work *home,* for the love of Mike! Then we ask him to sit down and program his job function. Boy! He thinks that's a terrible intrusion. But is it? If a manager takes 4BMAP training he will have 12 hours of in-class time to prepare P.M.P. items under the guidance of an instructor. He will probably prepare 15 or 20 items right in the classroom. After the training is completed he will go back to his job, and if he sets as his objective the preparing of one P.M.P. item per day, in six months he will have most of his job functions programmed. Of course, a P.M.P. is never completed because of new requirements being added, periodic changes, etc. Now, when he gets into the P.M.P. habit he will undoubtedly have a thousand percent more free time than he had before, and he will cover more bases than he ever covered in the past.

"If that isn't time saving I don't know what is. A thousand percent improvement in time availability! It sounds fantastic but it is quite true, and it is based on actual experience."

How to Make Your Subordinate Responsible for Your Promotions

"You say, 'on experience.' Has this actually been done?" I asked.

"In literally hundreds of cases. I wasn't kidding when I said I have seen job functions get so perfectly organized the position vanishes. How much time does that save?"

"Oops! We're back to lay-offs again," I chided.

"Recall what I said to that? I've never seen a man who got his job that well organized who wasn't transferred to another more important assignment. Half of the mid-managers who never seem to get promoted are shelved because senior management is permitted to think they can't be replaced. It's the man who demonstrates by his system, by his recorded operating instructions on each individual responsibility, by his care in seeing to it that someone is being groomed for his job and can take the job over, who gets promoted every time."

"I can buy that," I said, "but you said he can get so perfectly organized his position vanishes. What do you mean? How can a management position vanish?"

"It probably wasn't there in the first place. Somebody wanted a title and he got one. What he was doing before the title, he still does after it. When his job is properly programmed it is clearly revealed as an accountable function, not a responsible one. So instead of putting his job into P.M.P.'s, we put it into J.P.'s and quite effectively the management position vanishes. Now if top level management wants to call a clerk a manager, that's their business. But at least they will know what the man does."

"But the position didn't vanish. The title did, perhaps, but the position and the salary are the same," I observed.

"If management so decrees," he said with a shrug. "But do you know what usually happens? The man is now free to take on a real management assignment. With his accountabilities clearly defined, they can be added to Job Procedures of existing personnel and the management assignment just disappears. Naturally the affected manager is now free to take on a heavier assignment."

I interrupted. "Or has nicely cleared the way for management to fire him."

"Boy, you are determined to have people fired, aren't you?"

"I'm just facing a fact, Bob."

"No, you aren't. You are forcing facts. That man will be fired only if he is an incompetent; then unless you expect management to live with incompetence, he darn well should be fired."

"But," I insisted, "if you organize his job so that a

non-management employee can handle it, I say he *will* be fired. Or be declared redundant."

"Only if he is too incompetent to be moved into another management position."

"Would 4BMAP improve his competence?"

"If his competence was measured on administrative ability, I would say '*yes*' emphatically."

Strengthening Management Positions

"In other words, 4BMAP can organize a job so perfectly," I said, "and from what I've seen so far, it can do it, that it can cause a management position to disappear and yet make the incumbent of that disappeared position so much more effective that he would probably be internally moved to a heavier assignment. Will it do that?"

"Since you're setting up a hypothetical case I'll have to give you a hypothetical answer," he replied. "Yes, it will do that. Now to get rid of hypothesis and get down to facts, a man whose management function disappears through the installation of 4BMAP never had a strong management position in the first place. His title was probably the closest he came to the management function. However, what 4BMAP training will do for him personally is something else. It will give him a much different attitude. His confidence in his own ability will simply soar. He will get rid of fears. He will know how to use his skills instead of letting them lie dormant. He will understand a system that takes the worry out of management. In short, 4BMAP will give him support such as he never had before.

"Now here are the 'ifs' of the matter," he continued. "*If* he has the personality for the higher job. . . *If* he has the technical competence for the higher job. . . . *If* he aspires to the higher job. . . . *If* all of THOSE attributes and skills exist, he will *get* the higher job."

"And, if he doesn't have those attributes and skills?"

"Then management will probably declare him redundant, move him sideways, or retire him."

"And even I have to agree to that," I said.

"Good. And now that you're agreeing with me, let me say this. Management, thank God, is at last facing up to its responsibility to the mid- and junior manager. It now sees how its imposed changes in routine, methods, objectives, etc., have eliminated experience, past expertise and memory as the criteria on which a man can be judged. The most proficient mid-manager ten years ago has had to make astounding changes in his philosophies, skills and procedures. Most, if not all, of those changes were imposed on him by top management, government, etc., and top management must share the responsibility for the mid-manager who didn't or couldn't adjust to the changes. Rarely did it provide any kind of system to help him. The attitude was simply, 'If you can't stand the steam, get out of the kitchen,' and if that wasn't the attitude then the other method was to isolate the man, build departments around him, by-pass him. The consequence, of course, was redundancy or sideways promotions for the incumbent."

"Neither of which was very profitable," I added.

"Certainly not. In demoralization alone, the cost is terrible, and management must and is beginning to accept the bulk of the responsibility. It is looking for solutions. It has created a monster and it is looking for a dragon killer. I can't say all presidents are finding one, but they are at least looking."

"When you say management is responsible for the monster, do you mean it is responsible for the changes it has imposed which caused the monster?" I asked.

Dealing with Constant Change

"Exactly. Let me illustrate. When I became a division manager, and without going into a lot of detail, I made quite a few changes after I got the job. The president was also making changes. Even the government was making changes for the division, and so were the unions. In less than five years I couldn't begin to describe all the changes that were made."

"But they would all be a necessary byproduct of technological advance, wouldn't they?" I asked. "I mean, change is the only thing that's constant. Don't managers expect it?"

"Certainly they do. But expecting it and handling it are two different things. Because of the very volume of change, most managers are overloaded, often confused, discouraged and disorganized. They have no way of riding with the change, meaning no system by which change can be introduced. And top-level managers have begun to take notice and are doing something about it."

How to Avoid Wasted Training

"You mean they are sending managers to schools, seminars, etc.?"

"That's one thing, but they've been doing that for years. However, it's only the first step and if they don't take the second one, the first will be a waste of time and money."

"Of course," I said, "I can sense 4BMAP coming into the conversation!"

"You can be darn sure it is!" he laughed. "With this system an investment in training really pays off. Did you ever have an employee attend a course or a seminar, pay a lot for it, and in six months be unable to show you in action one single smidgen of what he learned? If I had ten cents for every twenty dollars industry has spent in sending their people away for a course that literally produced nothing for the company that sent them, I'd be a very rich man! I've seen men who have gone on six-week courses—in residence, where the fee alone is over $2,000, to say nothing about salary, travel and accommodation—and within six months they wouldn't have been able to get a mark of 20 if they had sat down for an exam on the course they took.

"But that's not the point," he hastened to add. "Remembering anything you learned six months ago is difficult for most . . . impossible for many . . . and it's not our fault! As I said before, the human mind theoretically may have unlimited capacity, but in actual practice—with, say 95% of the population—it is *not* unlimited. It is crowded! . . . crowded with detail, and no matter how hard you work at it, and no matter how many experts tell you that you can remember 100% more than you can *now* remember, the human mind *in practice* cannot retain the memory of a complex job function and a host of other things, including skills and techniques, that he might pick up at some training session."

"Not unless it was specially trained," I added.

"Agreed, but to get that special training you would have to go to a school where they wash your brains."

"Oh, come on, Bob," I argued. "There are many memory training programs in existence." (I personally didn't think they were worth the time or money involved but I wanted his reaction.)

"There are, I'm sure. All you have to do is check out the graduates of those courses six months after they leave the seminar room."

"I know. You ask them about the memory course and they say, 'What memory course?' Right?" I laughed.

How to Convert Classroom Knowledge to Job Station Proficiency

He lit a cigarette, sat down deep in the chair and began to think out loud.

"It's a shame," he said quietly. "When I think of the whole educational process I get a little discouraged. Kids are covering a lot of subject matter in grade school, high school and college—but they are applying less and forgetting more. Of course, you have to exempt trades skill training and certain professional skill training. I mean, a doctor doesn't have to learn over and over how to remove an appendix, or a C.A. doesn't have to re-invent a balance sheet. But in plain basic management skills far too little of what is learned within the educational system ever sees the light of day in actual practice.

"And again, it's not the *student's* fault!" he said raising his voice in emphasis. "And it's not the *teacher's* fault! It's the fault of there being a lack of system! Most business courses— M.B.A.'s, Bachelor Degrees in Commerce etc.— have a lot of valuable contemporary content. Those who do apply what they learn—and there are a few—give much to the management function. But the vast majority come into a job which top executives, policy boards, etc., have already laid out. The perimeters have been set, methods and techniques installed— perhaps antiquated but nevertheless installed. And the man either shapes himself to fit the mold or he finds himself toe to toe with some immediate supervisor who hasn't fired an original idea since he stepped off the ark!

"In the January, '71, edition of the *Harvard Business Review*," he said with intensity, "I remember reading an article called 'The Myth of the Well-Educated Manager.' If I recall it correctly, the author said the degreed person was not the most effective manager in the long run! Marks were not related to individual success. As I read it I found myself wondering why academic proficiency in the classroom apparently didn't do so well in the business office. I wondered if it was the academics or a lack of system through which the academics could be applied!"

"Well," I said, "if he applied what he learned as a commerce student, wouldn't he be able to *set up* a system?"

Applying Managerial Knowledge

"Depending on essentially two things," Bob replied. "One, whether he really learned a system—and I don't think any college, university, or school in the country (except Pepperdine University which teaches 4BMAP) actually teaches one as basically simple or as effective as 4BMAP—and two, whether he would have the personal freedom on the job to install the system. Much evidence exists to say he wouldn't.

"In consequence," he continued, "it's easy to understand why an academician is not necessarily a business or management success. If knowledge alone was a definition of management success, then a set of encyclopedia should actually make a good manager. And, of course, it won't. It is the *application* of knowledge that counts, and anything that is going to be *applied* must have a means, a system or a device for applying it. And I believe when it comes to administrative systems and techniques, the 4BMAP program cannot be beat," he concluded.

"In short, it's the vehicle that will carry the knowledge into the job function. Right?"

"*Right!*"

"But isn't 4BMAP also part of the knowledge factor?" I asked. "By that I mean you have to *learn* 4BMAP. You said it takes five days of training from a professional and perhaps four to six months for the manager to get fully programmed. That seems to me to be a lot of knowledge to acquire."

"Knowledge," he repeated. "Yes, but only in the sense that there is some knowledge involved in learning how to screw a light bulb into a socket, and knowing where and how to press the light switch. But not in the way of knowledge about electricity. 4BMAP will tell you how to press the buttons to make administrative knowledge work, but it isn't in itself administrative knowledge."

"In other words, it won't provide a management philosophy," I suggested. "It won't replace Management by Objectives or the Grid System, or a sophisticated accounting system. Is that correct?"

"That's correct; it won't. But I'll tell you what it will do. It will make those management philosophies and principles work. It will turn them on, so to speak. You won't be in the position of one who has screwed in the light bulb but is unable to find the switch or the handle."

Using 4BMAP with Other Systems

I started to think about a school division that was introducing P.P.B.S. (Program Planning and Budget Systems). It too was a management technique based on planning, budgeting, etc. I asked Bob if he had ever run into it.

"I most certainly have. It was going into one of our School Divisions. The cost of installation was upwards of $200,000. Some of the principals who were spearheading the installation happened to mention it to my associate, Dr. Pence W. Dacus, at Pepperdine University. He studied it, decided it was a good system but would become hopelessly bogged down at a certain point in the installation. Dr. Dacus went over it thoroughly and showed how a parallel installation of 4BMAP would make the system work. Without 4BMAP it was at best a hope that it would work, at worst a complete waste of thousands of dollars."

"Are they installing 4BMAP along with P.P.B.S.?" I asked.

"I understand that a group of the school personnel have been trained in 4BMAP. They in turn will, through the use of 4BMAP instructor and student kits, install the system in school districts. When this is done it will then be practical to introduce P.P.B.S. so that it will actually work."

"So, just to sum up," I said, "4BMAP is a system that can make systems work. It is, in effect, a system's system . . . right?"

"You are so right. It's a tool in the carpenter's hand . . . or the chisel in the sculptor's hand. It's a framework on which to build administrative expertise."

"O.K. Now I want to get back to Job Procedures," I said. "We've talked about them a bit because they are extensions of the manager's P.M.P. They dovetail. The manager's responsibility is outlined on his P.M.P. (Planned Management Program) but the accountable function being done by someone else is recorded in a Job Procedure. So let's talk about J.P.'s."

SIX

How to guarantee subordinate efficiency, involvement, and job satisfaction

"Briefly, Bob, how do you describe the purpose of a Job Procedure?"

"I'll give you the definition right out of the 4BMAP training program." he said.

1. To provide specific information on the *what, how, who* and *when* of a job so that efficient use of time and accuracy of work may be achieved.
2. To provide continuity and follow-through when assignments are changed.
3. To motivate personnel by letting them know precisely what is expected of them, when it is to be completed, and how it may be done.

"O.K., let's get down to the nuts and bolts of applying these purposes. Who makes up Job Procedures?" I asked for starters.

"Usually non-management personnel either on their own or in consultation with their immediate superiors."

"Can you spell out the fine difference?"

"Many secretaries, for example, know the details of their job accountabilities very well so all they need is instruction on the preparation of the forms. They can make up a J.P. without assistance except for occasional questions to their bosses. On the other hand, many of them need guidance and, believe it or not, *want* guidance in establishing step-by-step procedures. Half the secretaries in business today don't *really* know what their bosses want. With J.P.'s they at long last find out!"

"How come?"

"Because the boss outlines the step-by-step procedure he wants followed. It is recorded in the J.P. and there it remains for as long as the boss wants it to remain. There's no more guesswork ... no more mistakes made in ignorance and in innocence. The girl has an exact record of the manager's way of doing things. She may not agree with it, but if she is interested in keeping her boss happy, she at least knows exactly how to do her work to *make* him happy. Of course all secretaries add other details and bring some of their own creativeness to the job function."

What Is the Difference Between a Job
Description and a Job Procedure?

"It seems to me, Bob, that what you are really talking about are job descriptions," I observed.

"In no way am I referring to job descriptions," he said emphatically. "*These* are at the *best* a description of overall *responsibility*. Rarely are they descriptions of the job *function*. You can outline a person's responsibility ... describe it in complete detail ... but that doesn't mean you are outlining *how* or *when* or *who* in terms of his carrying out that described responsibility!" He was pretty warm and getting warmer!

"O.K.," I said, "I was just making an observation. Why so up tight?"

He laughed. "Didn't realize I was, but I guess I am at that. I suppose I've had a belly full of the administrator who takes hours and hours to work out job descriptions for his work force. Gets them all typed out and hands them out to each member and figures that from then on there should be no confusion on anybody's part. They know exactly what they are supposed to do. Their job can now be put in the category of a 'do-it-yourself' routine. But he forgets one thing. He forgets the routine!

"I've seen it often. A guy joins a company. Within ten minutes . . . and often before he even comes into work . . . he has a job description. Some of them are beauts! Two or three pages. They outline everything for which he is going to be held responsible and accountable, but he is told nothing about how to do a single job . . . when to do it . . . who to see to have it done . . . or what to do with it when it is done. This, the poor guy learns in the school of hard knocks and dismissals."

"Well, wasn't it part of the condition of his employment when he was hired?" I asked.

"I'm not with you; be more explicit."

"What I'm saying is, wouldn't management weigh his application against the demands of his job description and his expertise to carry it out?"

"I suppose they would. But what in blazes does *that* tell them? Here's a guy with a Masters in Business Administration. That's supposed to represent a lot of management knowledge. Now you hire this guy. In he walks and you present him with a job description! Heck, it doesn't even tell him where the bathroom is, when he is expected to arrive, what reports he is supposed to render and when they are to be rendered and how they are to be rendered . . . "

"And to *whom* they are to be rendered," I interjected.

"Exactly! You know how this man is going to get into motion? I'll tell you. By making mistakes, that's how. Just by making mistakes. By the hard knocks and lessons of trial and error . . . in *spite* of the fact that he's got the most beautiful description of his job that *his* boss could ever write. I'd like to

have a dollar or two for every job description that was ever
written and turned out to be useless.

"God love me," he growled, "I think job descriptions have
ruined more men than they have ever come close to helping."

"Wow!" I said. "You are sure agin job descriptions, aren't
you?"

The Shortcomings of Job Descriptions

"No, not entirely. I suppose they have *some* part to play
but I just haven't found what part. I've been witness to men
trying to get under control using their job descriptions as a
guide. In doing so they go right out of their minds trying to
relate the description to the procedure. Half of the time they
are the only ones who know *what* their job description is! They
don't publish them, you know. Their work group doesn't know
what the poor guy is held responsible and accountable for. I've
seen job descriptions prepared in which the manager preparing
them has carefully extracted all the drudge parts of his *own* job
and stuck them into a job description for some in-coming
subordinate, and then he expects the subordinate to carry out
details in a fashion the manager himself couldn't carry out."

"Give me an example," I asked.

"Easy. Here's a department head who has been authorized
to hire an assistant. He is asked to prepare a job description for
this new man. He does so. Included in the description is a
statement like this: 'The incumbent will be responsible for the
preparation of the department's stock inventory report. He will
check the report against an actual inventory count and render a
statement of overages and shortages.' That's all it says. Get the
picture? O.K. Now the guy is on the job. He wants to find out
what a stock report looks like. He wants to know to whom the
report should be sent. He wants to know how the inventory is
counted . . . what does 'shelf stock' mean . . . how is he to
determine whether there is a shortage or an overage? Where is
last month's inventory report? What day in the month is the
inventory taken? Does he do the count himself? If not, who

helps him? Oh! The questions are never ending. The guy's chance of doing an inventory report accurately is nil . . . absolutely *nil*!"

"The hard knocks of trial and error," I said.

"Exactly. The hard knocks. If that guy has a job description like that . . . and with maybe 20 or 30 assignments spelled out like that one . . . he will crack before he's there two months. More than that, while he staggers around the place trying to find out how, what, when and who, he is bothering dozens of other employees who are usually having their own troubles with their own job descriptions."

**How Your Secretary Can Handle Details
You Think You Should Handle**

"All right," I said, "you've made your point well. Job descriptions are virtually useless as a means of putting a new hire to work at a job station. You've talked about a new man. What about a new girl? Can you give me a couple of examples of how a Job *Procedure* would work . . . as opposed to a job description . . . for, say, a secretary?"

Examples:

"I can give you hundreds," he laughed, "but I'll give you a couple that you will think a bit corny. For instance, let me ask you this. Do you travel quite a bit?"

"Yes"

"Do you purchase your own flight tickets?"

"Yes."

"Do you make hotel reservations?"

"Yes."

"Do you have a secretary?"

"Yes."

"Then why are *you* going through all this procedure yourself? Haven't you got better things to do?"

"Never thought of it."

"Exactly. Many managers get the idea that this kind of assignment to a secretary makes them look lazy. They think it's more or less personal and they should be able to look after it themselves."

"Or maybe they are afraid of winding up in New York when they wanted to go to Toronto," I joked.

"Could be. But what would that tell you about the manager?"

"He's not too confident in his secretary."

"Correct. But why isn't he confident?"

"I guess he figures the girl has never dealt with airlines or travel agencies."

"And she probably hasn't. So what does that tell you?"

"I guess she should be taught."

"That would certainly help. But how would you teach her?"

"Tell her how to do it and audit her doing it, I suppose."

"Yep, that's what most managers do. Two months later you want to make another trip. Who will make the arrangements this time?"

"I probably will."

"Why?"

"It takes less time than telling the secretary how to do it all over again."

"Probably," he laughed. "Now what would have happened if you had helped her prepare a Job Procedure in the first place?"

"I wouldn't have to tell her all over again. It would be in her J.P. manual. Also, if I had to hire a new secretary it would still be there if she left."

"Excellent, you're learning fast," he smiled.

Author's Note:

In my secretary's J.P. manual you can read a page that explains just what did get recorded. This is how it reads:

a) When Mr. Shave is going on a trip he tells me what city he has to visit and when he wants to be there.

b) I phone the Travel Agency (688-0673) and ask for Miss _____. I tell her when he wants to arrive and return from his destination.

c) Miss _____ calls me back and gives me the Flight #'s that come close to landing him when and where he wants to be.

d) If there is a wide discrepancy in departure times I tell him so he can make a choice. If not, I place an order for the tickets.

e) If there is enough time the tickets are mailed. If not, I pick them up at the agency—#2, Bentall Centre.

f) I ask Mr. Shave his hotel preference. I make reservations and list hotel name, date and time of his arrival, telephone number and the daily rates.

g) I make up a flight plan, including hotel arrangements (copy attached) and lay it on Mr. Shave's desk along with the tickets.

h) If he is traveling out of Canada I go to the bank (location described) and obtain the equivalent of $50.00 per day for each day he expects to be absent, in the currency of the country he is visiting, and put it with the tickets for him.

i) I write to the person he is visiting, or if no time is available I wire to inform him of the flight particulars.

Note: Always add hotels of his preference in each city to the list below so after awhile you won't have to ask him which hotel he prefers.

More Examples:

"How about another example; Try for a real corny one this time," I said.

"O.K. Do you have an annual physical examination?"

"Yes."

"When do you have it?"

"November."

"Who makes the appointment?"

"My wife."

"Did she ever forget to make one?"

"Often."

"Often, why?" he shot back.

"Just forgot."

"No system?"

"No system!"

"Bob, are you suggesting that my secretary should have my medical check-up date in her Job Procedures?" I asked a little indignantly.

"I sure am. You admit your appointment is forgotten. You will also admit that it takes time to arrange the appointment . . . perhaps not much . . . but nevertheless, time. So why not have it recorded?"

"It seems, ah . . . petty, but I suppose you're right."

"I agree, it *is* petty, and in the beginning of your installation effort you are not likely to put things like that into the system. You've got hundreds of other things to put in there first. What I was trying to illustrate to you is this. The manager's purpose in life is to be responsible for his entire job function. His non-management personnel carry out the accountable part of that function. The more he can delegate this part, the more time he has for doing the things which, as I've said, he is paid to do . . . think, plan, innovate, improve, etc."

"Isn't that a little like passing the buck? I mean, I could probably organize J.P.'s so that I would wind up with nothing to do but sign reports and letters, answer the phone, and welcome the nice people as they come through the front entrance," I said.

"If you could . . . and I know you can't . . . but if you could . . . you are *right now* ready for a substantial promotion," he smiled.

"Or the bread-line!" I said in mock horror.

"Here we go again," he laughed. "Well, I won't play. If your job can be done by a secretary you should be on the bread-line!"

"You win, but let's be serious," I laughed. "How about the office manager who has 20 people under him and they are all doing different things? Should each one of them have J.P.'s?"

"Why not?"

How to Improve or Eliminate Procedures by "Straight-Line" Thinking

"Well, take an accounts receivable clerk. She is fairly highly skilled. She learns the company's system and she runs with it. Her job is almost routine. It, and it alone, keeps her busy all through the month. Hardly a variation."

"Have you looked at an accounts receivable job station lately?"

"Well, no, I guess I haven't." He had a knack for making me feel I just cut off the limb I was standing on.

Handling Variations in Job Functions

"You should. The variation in that job is plenty. In some companies repayment terms for the different accounts are enough of a variant to send the clerk straight up. But there are other variants in the system. Billing dates vary. Extensions on billings vary. Posting procedures can vary. Discounts for prompt payments vary. And then we get to collections and if the clerk is handling collections too, the variants can become pretty complex ... form letters, collection procedures, when is the account assigned to someone else, etc. etc. There are many such variants."

"And as you have described it, no end of potential confusion."

"You'd better believe it."

"I'm beginning to see how J.P.'s might handle the variants very nicely *and* cut down on some of the confusion," I agreed.

"It does every time. I've seen systems change simply because managers are forced to think in straight lines as a result of 4BMAP. As they think about a job station from an objective

point of view . . . in order to get the station programmed . . .
they begin taking note of existing procedures. After all, it's
these procedures that are going into the 4BMAP system. As
they analyze them in order to describe them as in a J.P., they
suddenly realize they are cumbersome, confusing. Many times
unnecessary steps are being taken, but in the day-to-day *doing*
process, no one takes a look at *how* it is done. When they shape
that station up for J.P.'s they invariably wind up with not only
a controlled, efficient process, but also an infinitely more
simple process."

How to Overcome Resistance to Change and Get
Subordinates Enthused About Job Enrichment

"O.K.," I said to hurry him along. "All job stations can be
J.P.'d advantageously. J.P.'s will save time. Perhaps a lot of
time. The question uppermost in my mind is, will the
employees cooperate in preparing J.P.'s? Won't they consider it
a lot of extra work without realizing what time it may save
them?"

"If the installation is forced on them, they probably will,"
he replied. "People will always resist something they don't
understand. Point out the advantages to them and the resistance
is nil."

"Do you think telling them they will save time is sufficient
advantage?" I asked.

"Not likely; they see *that* only as an advantage for the
company, not for themselves. What is really significant from the
employees' point of view is the accuracy that can be obtained
. . . the job understanding they get and the sense of accomplish-
ment they feel. Their self-confidence really soars."

I interrupted, "I think you're being wishful, but go
ahead."

"If that's being wishful, this isn't," he replied quickly.
"Every employee wants to feel useful. He or she wants to be
part of a team. They want to be fully utilized. Nothing drives a
worker crazy more than trying to 'look busy.' I don't care how

nonchalant they are about their job, their company or their boss. They hate having to *look* busy when they know they *aren't* busy."

"There would be a few exceptions," I reminded him.

"Damn few, when you talk to them," he said. "They *may* tell you a lie, but not likely. Don't kid yourself, they *want* to feel they belong and that they earn their keep."

"You sure must have a different group of employees down here than we have in Canada," I said, testing his conviction.

"Not one bit different," he affirmed. "But I'll tell you what the difference is *if* there *is* a difference. It's the way they are *managed.* Sure we have our slackers, as you would call them, and we've got plenty of them. But under the Job Procedure System the *slackers* even get better. They may still be slackers but they are pretty productive whether they are or not. We are not likely to change *them* but we *can* change the system they work under.

What the Employee Wants from the System

"So where does the change have to come from? The management! And the management must be responsible for setting into motion systems with which every member of a group can identify. The system must be such as to permit the employee to release his full potential, create to some extent the procedure he's going to follow, organize his own job station so as to eliminate confusion, annoyance, time-wasting practices. He wants to know his job is taped, that he can be free of it at the end of the day and know exactly where to start in tomorrow. He wants to know that he's not buried in the job; that his efforts contribute to the whole scheme; that he's promotable on merit and when he has demonstrated his promotability he won't be cut off because there is no one to take his place. And one more thing," he rattled right along, "he wants to have respect for his manager. He wants to know he's in full control; that he delegates but doesn't abdicate; that he knows what's going on all the time and keeps himself free enough to be able to know it; that he's not so buried in detail himself that he ignores the employee or has no time for him."

"Wow!" I said breathlessly. "That's quite a speech! Will Job Procedures do all that?"

"Not just Job Procedures," he replied with the same conviction. "The whole 4BMAP System. We've only talked about the first phase . . . P.M.P.'s. The other three are just as important."

How to Replace "Redundancy" with "Potential"

"O.K., before we get onto them," I said, "talk some more a- bout how J.P.'s can make it possible for a manager to know when he needs more people or when he should allow a few to go."

Bob smiled knowingly as he said, "With the accent on *how* he should know when to allow a few to go . . . right?"

"All right, you've got me pegged," I laughed. "I guess I am a bit of a nut on excessive work forces, although I sure don't like to contribute to the unemployment situation either."

"4BMAP doesn't like it either," he said. "If any system is going to keep people fully occupied *and happy,* it's 4BMAP! If it reveals redundancy in the process it will just as often reveal production potential."

"And without the need of expanding the force to obtain it, right?"

"Of course," he exclaimed, "and because I really believe that, having witnessed it many times, let's not talk about redundancy that provoked lay-offs. Let's talk about the employee who just voluntarily quits. Maybe he's really valuable or maybe he's redundant. It doesn't matter except that in one case the hole he leaves is likely to be filled by another new hire, and in the other the system itself will fill the hole."

How to Make the System Take Over a Job Vacancy

"O.K., tell me how the system will fill the hole left by a clerk whose job became redundant." I asked.

"Since the system revealed the redundancy, I can presume the employee who left completed a J.P. for his job functions (unimportant as some of them may be) before he left. The supervisor, foreman or office manager simply goes through the J.P.'s and picks out those assignments he wants to retain as part of his whole system. He now starts issuing pages of the J.P. to the remaining work force. Pretty soon the job function has been integrated into the other J.P.'s in the department and the job station simply disappears."

"It sounds too simple," I challenged. "Doesn't this get down to the stage where the remaining group members can be overloaded to the breaking point? I mean, why not cut a group in half and give the jobs to the remaining half?"

"If management had no way of knowing what the overload point was, the danger would exist," he replied. "But that can't happen when everyone is working with Job Procedures. The manager has only to look through a Procedure binder to know whether an employee can take on an additional assignment or not. But what is even more fascinating is to see employees taking on the assignments *happily.*"

"You've got to be kidding!" I exclaimed.

How Job Procedures Lessen Drudgery

"No, I'm not kidding! You're reflecting the old philosophy that people hate work and have to be driven to do it. It's outdated. People hate drudgery, confusion and time on their hands, or being over-worked because of poor procedures. They don't hate useful work at all." He paused for a moment in contemplation, then, "How do you feel after you have put in an unproductive, frustrating day? Not very good! Right?"

"Right, but I don't feel good either when I've been going flat out and still get behind in my job assignments."

"And that's exactly where the system comes in," he said enthusiastically. "First, it will expand the employee's discretionary time availability. Second, it will remove confusion at the job station. Third, it permits assignments to be varied. More than one person can do, say the drudge job, because they all work with Job Procedures. It only requires scheduling on the part of the office manager or supervisor to keep everyone rotating through drudge jobs. And fourth, because of Job Procedures, the output of an employee can be measured so that his job function completely fills his job time, no more, no less. And if I can add a final point, it's the opportunity to get some originality into the job by giving the employee an outlet for his own creativeness."

"So there would be no chance that the disappearing job station could overload the remaining stations?" I said with some skepticism.

"I wouldn't want to say 'no chance,' he hedged, "but there is a minimal chance of this happening. Some job assignments at various job stations cannot be so perfectly timed, or if they can be timed this month, the time factor might change substantially next month. But in a period of two or three months, the time standards will be established fairly accurately and adjustments of the assignments could be made."

"What you are getting at," I suggested, "is that with most managers, they only guess whether an employee can take on more assignments. They may guess pretty accurately but nevertheless they guess. With J.P.'s the guesswork is eliminated. Is that right?"

"Well no, it's not eliminated," he corrected, "but it is substantially reduced, and when it has been found to be wrong, adjustments can be made very quickly without going through extensive training exercises all over again."

"Like instead of *training* the remaining group member, do you simply hand him a page from a J.P.?" I asked for clarification.

"Just about like that. In fact, I would say that except for the highly complicated assignment which may need actual training, that's just the way it would go."

How to Put a New Employee into Production
in Less Than One Hour

"O.K., that looks after the redundant employee who leaves," I said. "What about the valuable one who leaves and has to be replaced?"

"If the new hire is not immediately available," he explained, "the remaining employees, with the aid of the supervisor, will have to temporarily take over the employee's J.P. and keep the job under control. That's exactly what is happening in my office right now due to the strike. My secretary is handling the J.P.'s of the personnel who are on strike and another management person, a woman, has been moved in to help her. They will have to continue to handle them until the strike is over. But they *are* handling them. The administrative work is being done."

"So when the replacement employee is eventually hired, he will simply take over the J.P. manual that has been temporarily handled by the remaining employees," I said. "Sounds pretty simple."

"It is pretty simple. That's what I've been telling you all morning. 4BMAP is simple . . . but it's also effective!" Big smile!

"But Bob," I pressed, "surely the new hire isn't going to take over the J.P. and be in business right away."

"Why not? Unless the manager has some special things to say to him or her, why can't they? My new secretary was highly productive on her first day. Anyone who takes over a J.P. can be productive immediately. All she needs to know is who is who, where's the washroom, when she goes to lunch (if these things aren't in the J.P.). What else does she need?"

I felt a little silly but said I guessed she didn't really need anything else. At least, at the moment, I couldn't think of anything else.

**How Recorded Procedural Changes Can Prevent
Critical Work Overloads**

"Now Bob, to change the subject a bit, what about the employee who comes to the boss and says, 'I can't keep up with the work!' "

"First, when there is no J.P. system the boss is removed from what he is doing while he tries to analyze the truth of the comment. Is the employee overworked, underskilled or simply unorganized? He has past experience to help him make the analysis but too often today, past experience has no relationship to the present condition. Again, things change. When *he* did the job or when so and so did it, it was easy to get it done in a specified period of time. But how long ago was that? And how many things have happened since then? How much additional volume is there? How many more procedures to follow, and so on?

"What is happening is this," he continued. "The boss must now analyze the job *after* the fact. And that is again like re-inventing the wheel. If the job had been analyzed, detailed as to procedure and recorded for visual examination, he would be able to measure its time magnitude and by making slight adjustments as they occur, he would never have to make huge adjustments when the problem becomes a crisis and someone is threatening a resignation because he feels overworked.

"With J.P.'s," he went on, "the job is outlined in writing, on a step-by-step basis. Each job assignment represents, say, a page in the J.P. binder. Suppose the procedure changes slightly. That change is recorded in the J.P. right now. Maybe a new J.P. item is written and the old one tossed out. Now the small change is already in the system and the incumbent has become adjusted to the change at once. As more adjustments are made to accommodate changes of policies, volume, personnel, etc., they are recorded in the J.P. The incumbent is always on top of the job!"

"That still doesn't solve the critical problem of the overworked employee," I reminded him.

"That's just it," he exclaimed, "there aren't any critical problems. They are faced down and corrected long before they become critical. That is precisely what the system will do. It will expose problems caused by changes long before the crisis."

How to Keep the Payroll Stable and Handle the Work Overload Too

"You had better run that past me again!" I said. "Suppose an accounts receivable clerk comes to you and says she can no longer keep up with the billings. She's falling behind every day. She's half out of her mind . . . on the verge of tears and a resignation. How will the J.P. prevent that?"

'Let's look at it from two points of view. One, there are no J.P.'s and two, there are. If there are no J.P.'s, what is the boss likely to do?"

"Hire an assistant for her, I guess."

"Exactly! Now we've expanded the work force. Problem solved? Yes, of course. But after the replacement has been on the job three months what do we find?" he asked.

"She probably hasn't enough to do to keep her busy," I guessed again.

"Right! So now we are into the 'make work' situation."

"Agreed, but at least the billings will go out on time and the receivables are current," I said.

"Undoubtedly, but isn't it strange that the accounts payable clerk, the receptionist, the filing clerk and perhaps the others in the work group are finding time on *their* hands. Why is *that* time not used to spread the load of the accounts receivable clerk?"

"Well, I suppose the office manager didn't think they had the time or, more important, the talent to do the receivables," I suggested.

"Right, on both counts. In the first instance, time availability: since there are no Job Procedures at their stations there is no way of really knowing how busy they are. And, of course, as for talent, because the accounts receivable clerk is working without J.P.'s, the time it would take to give her the talent would put the work back even further. So he hires an experienced accounts receivable clerk."

"Bob, I can't be sure, but I think you are forcing the solution," I said. "I think a manager would spread that work before he hired a new girl with or without Job Procedures."

"Let's say you are right. He tells the accounts payable clerk—probably the most talented—to take over the billings from A to K. Let's also say the payable clerk knows how to do the job. Now the billings are current. What do you think happens to the payables?"

"They get behind?"

"In all probability, they . . . "

I interrupted. "Now you are back to hiring a new girl to keep *all* the work current."

"Yes, I probably am. We have simply replaced the problem of the receivables with a problem in the payables, so we hire a new girl for the payables. Right?"

"Right, so what have we gained?" I asked.

"Nothing!" he replied and sat there waiting for me to say something.

"Well," I fell into the trap, "why not bring another existing employee, like say the filing clerk, into the payables?"

"Why not? Let's do that. Let's take the filing clerk and let her work on the payables. Now what happens?" he asked as though he knew he had me.

"The filing gets behind."

"Again, you are probably right. So now what? Hire a new filing clerk?" He was teasing now!

"I guess so," I said impatiently. "What would *you* do?"

"Well, it took a long time to get to it. What I did with you was make you realize that excessive workloads seem to have only one final solution . . . the engagement of more personnel."

"Is there any other solution?" I argued.

"There may, or may not be. The point is that management usually pursues only one course to solve that problem: hire someone. It may be an assistant accounts receivable clerk or it may be another filing clerk—but first or last, someone is going to be hired as an addition to the work force."

"O.K., what's the alternative you have?" I asked somewhat exasperatedly.

Integrating the Work Flow

"Job Procedures at every job station guarantee the full utilization of time. They also guarantee correct procedures, the elimination of confusion, and the integration of work flow. Everyone knows his own job but he also knows, or can quickly learn, the jobs of his co-workers. With this, portability is possible . . . one employee can take over another employee's job function temporarily or permanently. This makes it possible for critical workloads to be spread. It makes the manager's job a matter of scheduling. His decisions on work force needs may still persuade him to engage another employee, but he will have no doubt about the need for one and he will have no concern about having an employee bored because his time or talent is underutilized after he is engaged." It was spoken like a windup to a lecture on Job Procedures!

I let it sink in. It was quite a mouthful. I attempted the playback.

"So," I said, "it boils down to the fact that Job Procedures will see that everyone is fully employed, knows what he has to do, when, why, with whom, etc.; that all available time is harnessed for the isolated overloads and that each job station can be analyzed for the time demands that exist on each function."

"You're getting the message!" he smiled.

"I can see how this could work out pretty well for the absentee," I said. The system was now falling into place in my mind.

"Unquestionably. You're learning fast. The absent employee's job function can be covered by a co-worker's simply taking over the J.P.'s, and *that's* when you can spot redundancy pretty quickly. When everything is current and no one is putting in overtime despite an absent employee, you have redundancy."

"I know you've handled this question before, but don't you think—and be honest about this—that an employee would resist the idea of putting all of his procedures at a job station into J.P.'s?" I asked.

"If she thought for one minute it was your intention to use them so you could replace her, she surely would be reluctant. But as you already realize, that is not what the J.P. system is for, and I've yet to see an employee who fully understands its purpose show any reluctance to participate. Don't forget, each employee has added items, made rearrangements, and therefore considers the J.P. his own creation. In fact, each one is very proud of his handiwork."

I had to accept that explanation somewhat on faith. I decided to press on but hoped it would come up again.

How to Get Accurate Productivity at Once

"I know this is a pretty basic question, Bob, but give me a fast rundown on how J.P.'s are advantageous to the new employee and to the existing employee."

"O.K. Take the new employee. There are no J.P.'s in the office. Let's say a new clerk is hired. She arrives on Monday morning, apprehensive of her new boss and co-workers in the work group. She is introduced around, then the supervisor gives her a job to do. It's an easy one. She's eager and does it quickly. Now she goes back to the supervisor. He gives her another job. She does this one too but now she's been in the office long enough to see that the supervisor is pretty busy. In fact, just as she completes her second job she notices he is going to answer the phone and two people are standing at his desk. Is she going to interrupt? Not likely. She will probably talk to one of the girls, stretch the job she is given, or just sit down somewhere.

"She begins to feel like a fifth wheel already and wonders if the job will last and desperately tries to 'look busy' while she does nothing. Get the picture?"

"Yes, I've seen that picture many times," I assured him.

"Now, with J.P.'s she would spend her first hour going

through the binder getting an overview of her job responsibilities and some insight on the job accountabilities ... step-by-step procedures for each function. After that, she would discuss the job with the supervisor. He answers questions and away she goes. I can safely say I've never seen a new employee feel out of place with J.P.'s. She is productive within one hour. She is pulling her share of the load and she feels she is part of the team the very first morning. She is comfortable. The risk or fear of being incompetent is gone.

"That's why I know people do not need to be driven to be productive. They want to work. All they need is a system to help them," he insisted. "What they don't want is boredom, a feeling of uselessness, being an interruptive element in the office or having to look busy when they aren't."

How to Convince an Employee He Is Doing the Job Exactly as You Want It Done

"O.K.," I pressed on, "now what about the girl who has been on the job for years. What advantages do J.P.'s have for her?"

"The most important one I think is learning, at long last, just how her boss wants things done. I've seen secretaries for instance, who have worked for the same man for three or four years, sit down with him to work out a J.P. on some job function and, after it has been written up, discover that they've been doing it entirely differently than he really wanted it done."

"That sounds like a pretty unaware boss!" I said.

"Not really! Especially on minor things. For instance, how does his secretary answer his phone, greet a client in the outer office, keep his desk tidy, set up his letters, even serve coffee? I've known managers who sign letters and every time they do it they get a little annoyed because things are not as they really want them. Their title is not exactly right, or the paragraphs are block style instead of indented. Crazy, I know, but they live with it because it's too insignificant to really matter. When they make up a J.P. on handling correspondence, the annoyance is cleared up.

"I spoke before about a boss getting involved in detail," he continued. "It's done every day. Needless time losses in doing things others can do as well, or better. Here's a simple example. In the old days when I set up a meeting I used to call the personnel and invite them to the meeting. I would labor over an agenda and gather a lot of support files, operating manuals and so forth so that I'd be fully ready when the meeting started. Today, my secretary makes up most of the agenda by taking the headings out of my P.M.P. All I do is add a few current items. She informs those who are to attend when and where the meeting will take place, and sends out the agenda five days prior to the meeting. She has all support information gathered. Heck, I just walk into the room!

"It boils down to this," he said. "The girl with J.P.'s is no longer confused about what she does and is no longer guessing what her boss wants her to do or how it's supposed to be done. She is much happier and usually busier. I've yet to meet a secretary worth her salt who doesn't want to be busy . . . but they sure don't want to be confused! Nor do they want to do anything the wrong way over and over again."

I thought about a few I'd had over the years and I agreed with him.

How J.P.'s Reduce Demoralizing Criticism

"And here's something else," he continued. "I've mentioned it before. J.P.'s force the boss to think in straight lines about the job functions his employees have. He can no longer give them a job to do and say, 'just do it, you'll understand how, when you get into it.' Too often they don't, and when he gets it back, it's wrong and has to be done all over again. Who is to blame? The boss. But who gets the blame? The employee. No wonder there is hostility!"

"Couldn't that also apply to the mid-manager in relationship to top executives?" I asked.

"Definitely. Many a department head lives under a cloud of criticism . . . either stated or implied. It's demoralizing and it accounts for everything from the mass inter-industry movement of mid-managers that we see today right down to the last ulcer. Once again, I go back to the "Peter Principle."* He's right as far as he goes. But to me he is dealing with 'effect' and paying too little heed to 'cause.' *Why* will a manager rise to his own level of incompetence? The answer that seems to be overlooked is called *systems*—Management and Administrative Systems—which give the manager the means by which he can apply the competence he has."

I have disagreed with the Peter Principle on the grounds of attitude of the employee. Now Bob was disagreeing on the grounds of systems!

"If his company hasn't given him a vehicle to apply all the talent he has, is it the man's fault?" he asked. "Is he short on talent? The vast majority are not. Is a practicing surgeon short on talent? Only if he hasn't a scalpel. Is a garage mechanic short on talent? Only if he hasn't a monkey wrench. And is it any different for a manager? Not at all! If he doesn't have the tool—a system—to convey his talent, he might as well forget he has any. That's exactly what his superior does. He simply forgets the man has any talent and has suddenly reached his level of incompetence. His ascent in the company is instantly and forever arrested. It's a great shame, and companies are losing thousands of competent people every day by this exact route.

How a President Incorrectly Assessed His General Manager

"Listen," Bob fired right on, "I have a good friend who is the president of a medium-sized manufacturing plant. I had lunch with him one day and he was telling me how inefficient his general manager had become. Imagine! His general manager!

*The Peter Principle: Why Things Go Wrong, Lawrence J. Peter and Raymond Hull (New York, N.Y.: Morrow), 1969.

I asked him questions about their administrative procedures and he kept interrupting by saying, 'That's what's wrong with him, he's a poor administrator. Just a helluva of a salesman, but a lousy administrator. I shouldn't have given him the job.'

"I kept plowing in on procedures and systems," he continued, "and finally he said, 'So we don't have any systems. That's what I made the guy general manager for. I expected him to set up systems—but he's a lousy administrator. I'm going to have to fire him!'

"I was ready to explode and I said, 'What do you think the guy is, a genius? He has never been trained in procedures and obviously he never took over an installed administrative system. You yourself don't know an administrative system from flypaper. Yet, you're going to fire *him*. How doggone unperceptive can you get!"

Bob was reliving the conversation. His face was flushed and he was still smarting. "I told him everything I knew about 4BMAP, and he had it installed immediately."

Then he relaxed. "Well, to make a long story short, I saw that man again a week ago. What a difference! Thinks his G.M. is *tops*. Business was never so *good,* etc. And this was the guy he was going to *fire* only six months before!"

A New Look at Causes of Economic Regressions

We took a break. Bob had been answering questions for four hours and the last story got him pretty stirred up. As we sat there with our coffee he started to think out loud again—as though talking more to himself than to me.

"Suffering cats," he said quietly. "When I think about industry at large in this country it really concerns me. Most of the big companies are succeeding primarily because they have momentum and just enough to keep them viable in their market. Most of them are living with redundancy, empire builders and minimal productivity. The middle-sized companies get by on careful market selection, specialty production lines, rigid budget controls. The small companies depend on bank credit.

"But all the way along the line the condition common to them all is under-utilized talent by employees and managers. For the love of heaven, what could happen to this country if everyone—not just a few of the boys at the top, but everyone—used all of his talents, or, more precisely, had an opportunity to use them—a means, a device, a *system*! I'd bet a lot of money that productivity would soar and costs would go down. There would be millions more dollars available for expansion, unemployment would go down, prices would go down too. Well, maybe *they* wouldn't, but if they didn't, profits would rise like mad and the government would soon be out of the money-printing business! And *that* would be the end of inflation!! Also, the U.S.A. would again compete favorably in the foreign market because annual production improvements would equal or exceed annual increases in wages and the price of goods and services!"

He laughed! "That's a fast lecture in economics. I'll throw that in for nothing!"

Then he continued, "But seriously, our approach to the development of talent is basically wrong. I didn't say all wrong—basically wrong, big difference! We must of course continue to expand the levels of our talents, but equally important, industry must continue to find the means by which employees can apply the talents they already have."

How 4BMAP Unleashes Talent

"I know it's not your intention," I said, "to paint 4BMAP as the elixir of all company ills, but . . . " He interrupted.

"Of *course* it's not the elixir of company ills. As I said before, if the surgeon doesn't know *how* to remove an appendix there would be no sense giving him a scalpel. And if management doesn't know how to set up its books, develop its product, market its service, and do the myriad other things that make a company viable, 4BMAP won't teach them or help them. 4BMAP is simply the means by which this necessary know-how is fully applied. But I'll tell you this. Without 4BMAP unapplied talent is likely to be rampant with any company. And what does that tell you? Not that the company is in dire straits, on the verge of bankruptcy; no, not that. It tells you that in virtually every company on the continent there is untapped talent, potential galore, improved profits waiting to be earned. I liken most companies to race horses tethered to the starting gate. There they are, as genetically perfect as breeding can make them, trained from the day they were colts, groomed to perfection, but they aren't able to get out of the starting gate because of the tethers."

"And 4BMAP would cut the tether?" I said.

"Yes, 4BMAP would cut the tether. *All* the breeding, training and grooming would be unleashed, and *if* all that effort was done right, the horse *would win.*"

"In respect to a company rather than a horse, what do you mean *if* all the effort was done right, it would win?" I asked.

"Well, you can wreck a horse if you don't know how to train him. And you can wreck a company if you don't know how to develop it. What would be the good of having highly trained salesmen when the problem of production hasn't been worked out? Or having a large cash flow if you don't know how to make a bank deposit? Or working out a plant expansion if you don't know how to capitalize it?

"4BMAP by itself will not teach anyone the basic or advanced knowledge of corporate management. Its *only* function is to serve as a *means* for introducing and applying that knowledge so that every morsel of it can be brought to bear on the challenge of management. You can be the world's greatest expert on the subject of, as you say, Management by Objectives, or Communications in Management. You may be a systems engineer, an actuary, a chartered accountant, but if you can't bring to bear on your job station the full impact of your expertise, you are like the tethered horse. You won't go anywhere, and to the degree of your involvement in the company management function, the company won't go any-where."

"And so, the potential remains untapped," I summed up.

"Exactly. And with some companies that potential is greater than its owners would ever dream possible."

"And, 4BMAP would release it?"

"It sure would!"

"Why wouldn't a good kick in the pants do the same thing?" I asked.

Bob laughed at my impertinence. "It has been tried . . . and I'm sure you're one who has tried it. Did it produce lasting results?"

"No, I can't say that it did. But it sure had some immediate results."

"Like someone got fired, right?" Bob asked.

"Not necessarily. They just moved a little quicker."

"Where did they move *to*? You mean they did things *wrong* but *faster*. Is that right?"

Using "Foot Motivation"

"Oh, I wouldn't say that," I pleaded. "They knew their jobs. They just got lazy and a little foot motivation sort of spurred them on."

"For how long?"

"I know what you're driving at. The foot had to be applied quite regularly, is that it?" I asked.

"It sure is. I've never seen, as you say, 'foot motivation' last more than a week. Let down the pressure and you're back to square *one* again!"

"Well, how does 4BMAP replace the foot motivation?"

"Because it defines procedures . . . "

"They *were* defined," I broke in.

"Clearly, and in writing?"

"Clearly, but not necessarily in writing."

"That's the mistake . . . "

"How come?" I cut in again. "An accounts receivable clerk knows what she is doing. She knows the procedures. She just gets lazy!"

"Would you believe bored, more than lazy?"

"Perhaps. But how would 4BMAP reduce the boredom?"

"It gives her a complete picture of the operation. She understands how she fits into the whole scheme of things. Her function is clearly defined. She isn't isolated. She knows her job and she knows others can learn her job quickly. She's not boxed in. She *can* be rotated. On top of that, she can and does participate in developing the procedures on her job. She is actually taking on a teaching function simply by preparing her own J.P.'s. When we get to the other phases of 4BMAP you will see how she has open line communications with management. You will see how the system embraces every employee, makes them all belong, permitting them to contribute their opinions, their expertise and their creativeness."

"Bob, I admit what you have just said sounds pretty exciting. I think an employee can become that involved, *if* he or she is motivated. But if they lack motivation, will 4BMAP give it to them?"

"I'll give an unqualified 'yes' to that one," he said. "It is quite a thrill to watch it. As I've said before, the system gives the employee not just an understanding of his job function and a chance to participate in the development or the improvement of the function; it also gives him a tremendous lift in self-confidence, in decisiveness, in creativeness. These are the things that really constitute motivation.

"Now, having said that, let me also say that perhaps one employee out of a hundred will not get motivated, and here's what 4BMAP will do for that one. It will make it a whale of a lot easier to *fire* him!"

SEVEN

Advantages of the operating letter system

We had a light lunch served by Mrs. Babbidge who had been busying herself around the house all morning.

"I think you boys need a little food. From what I've heard from time to time you both sound as though you are burning up a lot of energy. My, but you're having a hot time in the old town tonight!" she laughed. "When do you expect to finish so we can all relax a bit . . . take a boat ride? Bob, you cut this short. Gordon has a right to a little of that beautiful sun we keep bragging about."

"Well," Bob replied, "if the guy would quit setting up obstacles I wouldn't have to take so much time knocking them down. He's a tough one to convince. But I think I'm winning. Agree, Gordon?"

"So far, so good! In fact, I must admit I'm pretty impressed with the whole deal."

"Well, as the man said, you ain't seen nuthin' yet!"

We finished the sandwiches, sat back with our coffee (there was always a pot available and Bob's cup was rarely empty), and I started the discussion by asking him how and why he developed the Operating Letter System.

How an Operating Letter Can Turn a Head Office Directive into a Job-Station Procedure

"In most large national companies you will find literally hundreds of manuals, guide books, handbooks of all kinds and descriptions; sometimes there are letters, memos, bulletins, magazines . . . a terrific raft of Head Office instructions. You might say they have a couple of Bibles, a few encyclopedias all written to tell management and non-management personnel what they are supposed to do to earn their keep and ply their skills and trades."

There was a twinkle in his eye as he said, "All good stuff, mind you . . . important stuff . . . but the volume of it! Man alive, it would take all your time just to read it to determine what applied to your specific job. Trying to find, say, a specific answer to a problem you might be faced with, usually took so much time that the problem disappeared before you got the answer. You would be plowing through chapter and verse that had nothing to do with the problem and often in doing so you happened across so many other things you had forgotten, that the thing you originally started to research got lost in a myriad number of things entirely unrelated."

He reached into his brief case and drew out a three-ring binder. He laid it on the table, opened it at random, and said, "Now here is an Operating Letter binder and that's an Operating Letter you are looking at." He turned the book around so he could read it.

"What this Operating Letter is all about is not important, but here's its purpose." He studied the top part of the page, looked quickly down the headings and then said, "Right, now I remember. This particular Operating Letter was written for the purpose of clarifying a Head Office directive. Not only does it clarify it, but it also relates it to one specific division. It puts the directive into language the people in the division can thoroughly understand. It names the job stations most affected by the directive and it spells out to those people what is supposed to be done, how it is to be done, who is to do it, when it is to be done, and finally, on occasion, why it must be done."

"Does it name the people by name?" I asked.

"Very rarely. Never, if possible. People change, get transferred, promoted, etc., and when they leave the station the Operating Letter binder stays right there. The new person simply takes it over."

"Who gets copies of an Operating Letter?" I asked.

"Usually all managers and most of the work force in the division," he replied. "It may not be sent directly to every manager individually, but they all have access to an O.L. binder. It may be at the desk of a district head, or in three-ring binders centrally located in a work group. It doesn't matter, except that they all have access to it, *including* non-management people who may want to refer to it.

"Would anyone get it by direct mail?"

"Oh sure," he smiled. "Usually all managers in the division. However, O.L.'s written on a specific subject may only involve district managers, so *that* O.L. is forwarded only to them."

"Would district managers have an Operating Letter System that they put out for their own people?"

"Yes, they would. The purpose of their O.L.'s would center fairly well on instructions they wanted followed by the people in their district that were not already covered by the division O.L. System. These would be directives originating at the district manager's desk, or out of a personnel meeting he might hold . . . any number of sources."

"Would, say, a foreman or some other mid-manager below the level of a district manager issue O.L.'s?"

"Not, perhaps, in the same quantity, but yes, they could issue O.L.'s for the particular people within their management jurisdiction. Usually, O.L.'s are not written by first level managers because their instructions are generally placed directly into the Job Procedures of their non-management or subordinate personnel. However, in some cases a first line manager may have need for an O.L. System and there's nothing to stop him."

"Boy, that sounds like a lot of paperwork," I challenged.

"Not really. In fact, the use of the O.L. System by levels of management *eliminates* paperwork. Think about it. Here's a little example. Say a Head Office directive is asking for a report that should arrive at the Head Office on the 25th of each month. The report is the responsibility of, say, a division manager. But they know the division manager is not going to produce the report himself. He's going to delegate that responsibility. O.K., how is he going to get people in motion?

How to Avoid Instruction Errors in Communications

"Well, he has a couple of choices," he went on. He can call a meeting of his district managers. But they are busy people so the question will quickly boil down to 'when can I get them together?'

"But assume he holds *regular* meetings. On the next one he brings this up. He reads the directive. He hands out copies. Six guys start scratching their heads. 'What the devil does it all mean?' they are asking. Sometimes they ask it out loud, but most times they say nothing. They don't want to reveal themselves—figure they'll read it again when they get back to their desks.

"The meeting ends and away they go. Assume they get right on it—and most *intend* to do so but back at the desk they find their priorities are all fouled up. There are fires to put out—but let's assume they forget the fires and dive into the directive. In time, after the telephone calls, etc., asking questions, they will see what part they have to play in getting the report together. That usually means the second level managers have to be put in motion. How do we do that? Call a meeting? O.K. Call a meeting. Then what happens? Copies are distributed and by then 50 to 60 guys scratch *their* heads as a result of *this* meeting.

"And so it goes. If the report requested gets out any time close to the date requested, the Head Office is lucky!

"What's the alternative? Letters. O.K., the division manager writes the first one. District managers get it and *right now* there are questions to be answered. The phone starts ringing and the division manager is tied up for hours. Soon he realizes that his letter left much room for doubts and confusions. He writes another letter to clarify the first one. Then the district managers start writing him memos—they don't want to *phone* again. So the division manager replies to these memos. *Paperwork*! It's like confetti—and when the district managers finally understand it they write letters to their second level managers and they in turn, write to the first level foremen, and the paper war starts all over again, only *this* time we've got 60 people writing letters to the second level and district managers who don't have time for it, and everyone is about to blow a fuse!

"Now compare that to the Operating Letter System." He paused, took a deep breath, swallowed and plowed on. I didn't realize it, of course, but he was setting me up for a first class lesson on communications.

How an Operating Letter Works

"Because of the format of an Operating Letter, nothing is left to chance. The explanation is perfectly clear because in the preparation of the Operating Letter the manager would have his sub-managers write it from the viewpoint of the recipients, and it must cover the *what, how, who* and *when* of the subject ... sometimes the *why* of it as well. And, of major importance, the *when* and title of the person who will review the O.L. for changes or cancellations.

"This is one package," Bob continued. "From it the entire work group will know what the Head Office directive is all about, what they must do, when it is to be done, how it is done, and who will do it.

"There are no meetings, no memos, telephone calls, letters or confusion. If sub-managers are expected to do something the O.L. will tell them and they will write the follow-up P.M.P. items for their P.M.P. binders. If a non-management person has to do something he will write up a Job Procedure and it will go into that J.P. binder.

"So there you have one procedure in writing. It clarifies the directive, puts the responsibility for it in the picture through P.M.P. items, and puts those who are accountable in motion through J.P. items."

The speed of his delivery had been accelerating with almost every sentence. He paused for a short breath and fired right on. "And this is another point: the person who may replace the person will also be able to do the job as it was laid down. If he's a manager he will take over the P.M.P.; if a non-manager, he'll take over a Job Procedure. You see, no re-invention of a lot of wheels."

How to Examine the Components of a
Letter or Memo

Before he could get another word in I jumped into the fray. "Hold on just a darn minute," I requested, "that's a lot of mouthwash to gargle in one gulp. Let's start over again. A directive comes out from Head Office. It tells the division manager that from this date forward he's responsible for sending in a report. It involves the whole division. It must come in on the 25th of the month. The report has to be compiled so a lot of people in the district offices and below are involved in its preparation. The division manager sends out a letter. The letter isn't clear and triggers off a lot of questions. Why isn't the letter clear? Can't that division manager write a clear letter?"

"If it's a clearly defined subject, is uncomplicated, and deals with a one-time situation . . . where you get the letter, do it and forget it . . . he can. But if it contains more than one subject, more than one directive, more than two or three steps to implementation, and must be repeated at periodic intervals, you can be sure it is going to be misunderstood and will create a lot of unanswered questions."

"All the time?" I queried.

That made him stop and think for a moment, and he said, "Most of the time." There was a short pause. "But it only has to happen *once* for a lot of confusion to develop and a lot of time to be wasted."

He snubbed out a cigarette and rattled right on. "You may ask why the directive from Head Office can't stand on its own. Why not just hand out copies to everyone, let them read it and get it over with?"

I started to say, "Yeah, why not . . . " but he burst right in with his own answer.

Overcoming the Problems Posed by Directives

"The directive has been sent to every division in the company. It will rarely cover all the questions it creates at the various division offices. For instance, it rarely names the job stations that are going to be involved in the preparation of, say, the report we are talking about. It may . . . and it would be an exception if it did . . . mention the stations at the *division* office but you can be sure it won't mention them at the *district* level or any other level below the district . . . and that simply means it won't cover the details involved in gathering together the information from which the report will be compiled. It won't make reference to certain laws or conditions that exist in any particular division which makes the gathering procedures slightly different between divisions. It won't say what district is to do so and so, and after doing it, what they do *with* it—like what station in the division office gets what they get, and what the station does with it when they get it."

I took a breath as if I was preparing for my turn to speak, but no turn came.

"I know what you're going to ask. You're sitting there saying, 'Well what is a division manager for? He should be able to interpret the directive,' right?" I wanted to say something but had no chance. He bashed right along. "Well of *course* he is responsible for the interpretations. But how does he disseminate his *interpretation?*" Again I tried to get the word-wedge in but before I could even clear my throat . . . "He calls a meeting, and as I've said before, that will cause more questions or create more confusion and paperwork than if he had sent copies of the directive to them and let them figure it out."

"Well," I tried to say, "why not send . . . ?"

Letters and Memos vs. Systems

"A letter? A memo?" he beat me again. "What have I said about that already? Aside from triggering off reams of paperwork in solving confusions, don't *ever* forget the incidence of lost, mislaid or misfiled letters and memos. You wind up getting the report . . . miraculously . . . the first month, but what happens on the second and subsequent months? Do you think a complicated report can be done the second time without having some sort of a guide? Hardly a chance! If the memo or letter is misplaced, that report won't get off the ground the second time. And even if it *isn't* misplaced, how will the people know the report is due again? What are they going to use as a reminder that it has to be done each month?"

"I would imagine," I said quickly, "they would use an abey . . . "

"An abeyance file? A tickler file? Is that what you were going to say?"

"Well, yes, what's wrong with that?"

"Maybe nothing—as long as they *remember to look* into the abeyance file or check the tickler file. "But this lasts only so long. They forget to look into the files, or if they remember to do so they remember too late. More than that, what happens when the people who are accountable transfer, or are promoted, absent, fired? Will *their* successors know about the abeyance files, and even if they did, do you think they won't have to re-invent the step-by-step procedures for doing the report? How much time will that lose for the new incumbent? Even the one who made it up the first time will, if he or she doesn't have a Job Procedure, have to go through the learning process all over again in order to make it up the *second* time. In fact, the re-inventing process could go on for five or six months just to get the *first* person locked into the procedures so that memory alone looks after the report's preparation. And, don't forget the numerous telephone calls back and forth while people are getting re-educated!"

While Bob poured another cup of coffee he just kept on talking! "No, the memo, letter, abeyance file system is loaded with potential trouble. So are meetings, by the way. But letters are particularly bad. They're only good for one-time situations. No life span at all. No letter should be written that can't be destroyed after it has been read and the instructions carried out. I was *continually* putting on the bottom of my letters, 'This letter should be destroyed when implemented but not later than . . . ,' and I put a date in there. It saves a lot of the company's investment in filing cabinets. If anything is important enough to be kept it is important enough to be embodied in a system, instantly available for reference, numbered in sequential order, indexed for quick identification and clearly marked for updating."

How to Avoid Negative Results
from Faulty Communications

With that last burst I decided enough was *enough*! He had my brain fogged up pretty thoroughly and if I was going to understand this system at all I had to slow him down. "Bob," I said, 'you've gotta stop for a bit and let me catch up. You've been talking like a machine gun on rapid fire. What the heck does all this mean in simple language?"

Bob started to laugh. "Finally!" he said between chuckles, "I . . . ha! ha! . . . I was waiting for the explosion. Ha! Ha! I *knew* you were about ready to blow your stack." He threw his head back and laughed heartily!

"Did I miss the humor?" I said even more confused.

"You . . . ha! ha! . . . you should see your face!" He wiped away a tear that had broken surface. "I'm *sorry*, Gordon! I've had some fun at your expense."

I was still in the dark. I hadn't found it funny at all.

"This is exactly what happens at a meeting," he said, still trying to control his laughter. "You look like the typical manager in a management meeting after the boss has delivered a long, complicated directive. The way you look is the way most managers look after the boss quits talking . . . confused, annoyed, stunned! I couldn't have made my point better."

"*What* point?" I demanded.

Interpretation and Confusion

"The uselessness of a meeting for conveying complicated directives," he answered. "This wasn't staged, believe me. What I said to you was all fact and truth. Everything is pertinent. Yet, I'm sure you are pretty confused about the Operating Letter System. And it's a *simple* system. Imagine what happens in a meeting where the boss tries to get across a really complicated process! Or, how about the complicated company manuals? You have to hire an attorney to *interpret* them!"

"I'm beginning to get the joke," I said.

He laughed again and between chuckles tried to make his apologies stick. He hadn't intended to carry it quite so far, sorry he made me angry, etc.!

"O.K.," I said, "you made your point. Meetings aren't so good for conveying complicated directives . . . "

"And neither are letters," and the chuckles started over again. "If I put all of what I said in a letter, would it be any clearer?" he asked.

"Perhaps not, but at least I'd have it in my hand to go over it again."

"And that's the only thing you can say about a letter that *could* make sense. But *does* it? On the assumption the letter creates confusion, I agree that restudying it may reduce the confusion. But will it *eliminate* it? Not very likely. Wherever there is an ambiguity in the letter there is *no* way that restudying it is going to clear it. The ambiguity is not recognized by the author. *He* wasn't ambiguous when he wrote it. He didn't even think of the possibility of his comments creating an ambiguous impression. It's only when it gets into the hands of the receiver, gets *his* interpretations, that ambiguity sets in."

"I know. Unless that ambiguity is clarified, no action can or will be taken," I said, getting into stride with his recovered composure.

"Of course not. If the action *is* taken there is a 50/50 chance it will be wrong. That's pretty tough odds. And if the odds are ignored, the instructions guessed at *and* implemented and turn out to be *wrong,* guess who gets the blame? And who has to do the report over?"

"The poor jerk who guesses wrong," I answered.

"Correct!"

How to Guarantee the Effective Transmission and Reception of Directives

"O.K.," I said with some determination. "Let's get back to the Operating Letter System. What's it all good for?"

"Well, here it is. Right from the course itself," he said. "The objectives of the Operating Letter System are as follows:

1. To standardize the dissemination of local policies and procedures.
2. To provide a means for rapid identification of specific instructions by all personnel.
3. To provide periodic updating or cancellation when personnel assignments change.
4. To improve overall efficiency, motivation and employee morale."

"It's beginning to get a little clearer," I said half in doubt. "Why didn't you say that in the first place?" I chided. (Actually

it wasn't clear at all but I didn't want to reveal my ignorance. And as I thought about it, that was exactly what
he said *would* happen. No one wants to *declare* his own
ignorance.)

"Because," he said smiling, "that's the way most managers
give their instructions or educate their employees. *They* know it
so well, they can't teach it. They assume too much. They *forget*
too much. They have no track to run on so they run all over the
map. That's exactly what I did with you in the last five minutes.
I intentionally assumed you knew things you obviously didn't
know and it made learning them very difficult for you.
In fact, if you didn't ask the questions you are asking,
you wouldn't know a *thing* about this system. But that's
exactly what is happening in industry. No wonder we have
fouled-up procedures, mistakes and customer hostility. No
one is asking questions! People function in ignorance, and
employees particularly hate to reveal their ignorance, and
it goes undetected until something is hopelessly screwed
up!"

"Agreed!" I said enthusiastically. I felt relieved to know I
wasn't dense. "I'm glad you don't mind the questions. But why
can't other methods of communication work just as well as an
Operating Letter? I think most interoffice directions are
presently handled by letters, memos and bulletins. What's
wrong with them exactly? Why can't I write a letter to a branch
manager and tell him to do something or ask him to send me
something without it getting things in a jackpot?"

"You *can* write him letters," he emphasized. "And with or
without the O.L. System you *will* write him letters and memos.
You will also write to customers, suppliers, government offices,
and a host of other correspondents of one kind or another. And
while these letters tend to have a longer life than interoffice
memos or an oral instruction, they invariably have fairly
predictable terminal dates. When the date arrives the correspondence should be buried."

**How to Create a Vastly Improved
Retrieval System for All Directives**

"Usually it *is,* isn't it?" I asked, thinking about the large filing systems most offices have installed.

"Yes, but too often it's in an unmarked graveyard," he answered.

"Now you're talking about *retrieval* systems."

"And well I should. Correspondence can be buried and not recovered and that's bad. But when *directives* get the same treatment, that's chaos! What is happening in too many companies is this. Management directs the affairs of the company by manuals, handbooks, etc., and *subordinate* managers implement the directives by using letters or memos as *their* medium for transmission. Serious decisions are being conveyed by mid-management to non-management personnel, by oral instructions or by writing memos, letters or bulletins. They should have permanence—a long life span—but they don't because somebody will read them (and forget them) and then bury them in the unmarked or badly marked graveyard.

"When things go wrong senior management screams, and out go the memos: 'Why don't you read my memo of such and such a date? It explains the procedure perfectly.' And the poor guy says, 'What memo? I didn't get any memo on this. Hey, Miss Secretary, the boss says he sent us a memo on this, do you remember getting it?' If she says 'yes' she is serving him well but it is not until she *retrieves* the memo that she is serving him *at all.* How much time do you think she will lose in the graveyard? Hours! And if you don't watch it, you'll find your whole work group looking for a missing memo! How much time does that represent? And again, how about the telephone calls?

"The vast majority of this dilemma is due to a lack of system—a down-to-earth nuts and bolts system that doesn't require an M.B.A. to follow or use. We call it the O.L. System, and it carries all permanent or semi-permanent directives. They do not wind up in filing cabinets. They go into three-ring binders and they are as important at the job station as the desk, chair or bench, and what's more, they are just as fixed." He paused a second, then ambled right on.

"Because they are instantly available, indexed for fast reference, nobody needs to be remembering regulations or procedures. They are right at everyone's finger tips. And what's just as important, they can be trusted to be accurate and current because each one is clearly marked for the date it will be reviewed and updated and who will do the reviewing and updating."

"You only took two breaths to get that out," I laughed. "Why don't you talk fast?"

"Sorry, Gordon," he replied, "I'm still proving to you that instruction verbally given is not easy to follow."

How to Get Your Subordinates Involved

"By way of summation, then," I said bravely, "the Operating Letter System provides a manager, at any level, with the means by which to make local interpretations of national directives, to issue detailed instructions on issues originating at his desk, and each Operating Letter is standardized as to format so that the writer doesn't miss the vital points such as *what, how, who, when,* etc. And the recipient knows how to read the O.L., how to file it and where to file it, who will update it, and when it will be updated. How do you like that for a good summation?"

"Pretty complete!" Bob complimented, with some amazement.

I nearly broke my arm patting my back. Not all verbal instructions are lost!

"Is the system easy to install?" I pressed on.

"As simple as any system of this importance could be. In fact, I've seen this system replace complex systems because it is so easy to install and produces such excellent and immediate results."

"Well, I'm still not convinced that your system is so simple," I said. "It seems to me that a lot of people are going to be issuing orders using Operating Letters to do it. Isn't there a danger of each level of management 'doing his own thing,' so to speak?"

"I sure hope there is," he replied with confidence. "Each manager at each level should be able to issue directives and orders to make his management function easier, more creative, and because he is usually on the spot, a whale of a lot more productive."

How the Operating Letter System Works

"But aren't you getting a massive amount of directives floating around the place?" I insisted. "I mean, if the division manager issues O.L.'s to his people, and district managers issue O.L.'s to their people, and then the supervisors have a go at it, aren't you going to drown the poor guy at the bottom with Operating Letters?"

"Doggone it, you don't understand the system, do you?" he said with some disappointment. "Look, here's how it works. Let's say I'm the division manager. And let's go back to the example of Head Office asking for a report. I bring in my immediate management people and we discuss this directive. We get as many of the bugs out as we can. We may pull in one or two district managers and get *their* opinions. We may even go to the first level of management and get *their* opinion."

"Do you, as division manager do all that?"

"On occasions I might, but usually not. I have sub-managers who will ferret out all answers that we can't come up with in our first meeting. Now, when we have the answers, know exactly what system we want followed, what stations are going to be involved, one of my subordinates drafts an Operating Letter. I look at it, make suggestions for changes if I see where a change should be made, and if necessary I might . . . and I often do . . . send it to one or two district managers to get their comments. When it has been thoroughly examined and changed, and is ready for implementation, my subordinate prepares the finished O.L. and I apply my signature. It is *then* sent to those on the distribution list. This would include the district managers, every major job station in the division, and special people in the division office management group. In short, all the members of the group on the distribution list either get a copy of the O.L. or have ready access to it at their job station."

"So the district managers never touch it? Never alter it for their own district offices?" I asked.

"Why should they? They participated in the preparation of it in the first place. If they wanted anything added they had the opportunity when they received the rough draft. No, by the time the O.L. is written we are about 98% sure that it is right, that it will be understood, and that it can be implemented without confusion."

"Would the O.L. tell each one just what he had to do?"

"Not only tell him, but it would instruct him, or *them,* to make up P.M.P. items to make sure they do it correctly and have it in the system so they will always follow it up on time and accurately, and it will tell managers to make sure Job Procedures are prepared so that those who carry out the accountable functions know exactly how to do it, etc."

"And all of that can go into an O.L.?" I asked dubiously.

"As I said, the guide is *what, how, who, when,* . . and if you write the O.L. with this guide in mind, you make very few errors or omissions."

The System at the District Level

"Don't district managers write *any* O.L.'s? I asked.

"Of course they do. I've already covered that," he answered rather curtly. "They have things come up in their offices which have nothing to do with the division office. The district manager is constantly on the lookout for ways to improve his district. When we get to the Detailed Job Inspection System you will know what I mean. When he discovers something that needs to be changed, or wishes to issue an instruction, he will do exactly what the division manager does ... call in his immediate subordinate managers, discuss the problem, come up with a solution, and send it out through the district manager's O.L. System. Of course many O.L.'s can be prepared by an individual without the necessity of holding meetings."

"Would all the job stations in the district get his O.L.'s along with the division manager's O.L.'s?"

"Sure, but they would be in different binders. The division manager's O.L.'s are clearly marked as such and are filed in one binder while the district manager's O.L.'s are filed in *another* binder."

"Sounds like a lot of O.L.'s," I suggested, rolling my eyeballs upward.

"Wrong! The division manager's binder is the main one and has the largest number of O.L.'s in it. The district manager's binder would have a lot fewer but they would all be just as important to the district personnel. Also, the second level manager must issue local instructions, so *he* has an O.L. System. But at this level there are fewer instructions of this type to be issued, so the second level manager's O.L. is not very thick."

"How about the first level . . . the foremen, for instance?"

"They rarely have an O.L. System for their work group ... although as managers they *might* use them. What happens is this. When they receive a division manager's O.L. they can identify from it just what they are supposed to do. They would then make up a P.M.P. item and with that they would have control on their responsible function. Then they would see that Job Procedures are made up so that the people who will be accountable have the means for step-by-step implementation. So they are using J.P.'s instead of O.L.'s for their work force, and they use P.M.P. items for their own reminder system."

How a Head Office Directive Can Be Understood by Every Person in the Work Force

"O.K., let's recapitulate," I said. "Let's see how verbal instructions are going! As a division manager you would analyze a Head Office directive; have some subordinate managers, maybe a district manager or two, examine the directive; and out of all that research you have a subordinate write a rough draft of an O.L. This would be circulated among your district managers for comments. With these you have the final O.L. prepared and out it goes to all job stations. The subordinate managers who get it read it to see what they have to do. They make up P.M.P. items so they will have the directive locked into their own system. They would also see that non-management personnel who are involved in the directive make up Job Procedures so that the accountable functions can be carried out. How am I doing?"

"You're doing great!" Bob replied enthusiastically.

"When district managers find something that strictly relates only to their own district they would write an O.L., and I suppose it would be written the same way . . . research, rough draft and the final product. Right? And the same with the second level managers?"

"Right!"

"The first level . . . the foremen, for instance . . . would not normally write O.L.'s. Instead, they would take out of the O.L.'s their bosses issued whatever instructions they are required to have and then make up P.M.P. items for their own binders. They would also see that J.P. items were prepared by those people who will actually do the implementation work."

"Exactly. So you can see now, I'm sure, how a directive originating out of Head Office can be interpreted, conveyed, and controlled right down to the person or persons who are responsible and accountable for carrying out the details of the directive," he said.

"And because it is written up in P.M.P.'s and J.P 's there is hardly a chance of it not being done right, and on time, month after month after month," I said with rather exciting awareness.

"Dead on! You are getting the picture perfectly," he exclaimed.

How to Make a Company Operating Manual
Work in Your Branch or Department

"That's encouraging, Bob. Before you swell my head too far, what is there in an O.L. that makes it so substantially different from, say, a company operating manual?"

"Quite a number of things," he answered. "If you study the average company operating manuals you invariably see page after page of policy, objectives, do's and don'ts. They are usually information oriented. But when they come across as action oriented they are not very specific. They lay down policy air-tight, but rarely do they interpret the policy so that the work force can understand the specific part *they* play and actually *perform* the work without additional instructions. Sometimes this is just bad communication skill on the part of the author, but more often it is the very nature of the manuals. They are issued to too wide an audience. The man on the bench or the girl at the desk, many times is just not interested. The worker won't plow through a company manual because it is usually too difficult to find the one required. Even managers find it a boring reading exercise even if they *can* find the proper one." He paused for emphasis.

"As a general rule they find out what's in the manual *after* something goes wrong and it is then brought to their attention . . . the hard way! On top of that, the manual is rarely job station oriented. Even if it is read it is hard to figure out how it should apply to one's own job station. The consequence is this: the work force thinks it pertains to someone else, not to them personally.

Shortcomings of a Company Manual

"And of course, one of the worst aspects of the company manual is its obsolescence factor. You can pick up any manual in existence and you will find it is full of directives that have been superseded by some other directive, or are so outdated nobody can believe they are still operative. The result? In some cases people do not trust the manual. To them it is *all* outdated."

"I must admit, on experience, they often seem to be," I agreed. "But aren't company manuals really prepared for management personnel? I don't think they were ever meant to be read by the general work force even though they are often available. On second thought, many of them contain instructions for non-management people," I added.

"Well, doesn't that take us back to just what I've been saying?" he stressed. "It's up to the local manager to see that the manual *is* read and understood. He can do that best by reading it himself and passing it on to his people through the Operating Letter System when required to do so. Then the directive is identified with someone they *know* and it is interpreted for their individual and collective benefit. Also, the O.L. will make reference to company manuals where required so people can find a specific one in a hurry if needed."

"Very good," I said quietly. "And I suppose the same thing applies in those companies that haven't got manuals and do all their directing orally or with letters and memos. Right?"

"Of course. The manager beneath the level of the issuing authority has to translate the instructions he receives in some way for his group who will then carry out the directive."

"Or the manager carries out the instruction himself," I added.

"That often happens. It's such a lot easier to do it than to explain how to do it to someone else. Once again, he is assuming the responsibility *and* the accountability."

"Well, you wouldn't use an Operating Letter to translate the directive that is, in effect, a one-time situation, would you?" I asked.

"Of course not!"

"What would you use?"

"As I said, a one-time situation can be covered by a memo or letter simply because it has a limited life span. The guy who gets it acts on it right away, and once it is done the memo can literally be thrown away."

"But if he had to do the same thing every month for a year, it should go on an Operating Letter, right?" I asked.

"You are learning slowly!" Bob was laughing.

How the Mid-Manager Can Positively Guarantee
Follow-Up by His Subordinates

"O.K.," I continued. "Now that we've handled Operating Letters as they apply to the interpretation of a Head Office directive or memo, let's talk about them as they pertain to the mid-manager who has an idea or two at his own level which he wants to pass on to his work group. Say, for instance, he wants to lay down a new rule to be followed. How does the O.L. fit that application?"

"Like a glove!" Bob replied excitedly. "You say a new rule . . . it could be a rule, a procedure, a policy, a marketing plan, cost control procedures, an organization chart, a building security plan, vacation schedules, new government regulations . . . it's unlimited.

"Just think of a small company for a minute." He paused to let the picture set in my mind. "It rarely has what we've been calling a company manual, a policy guide, or any other means by which to convey important management directives. Most of them do it by a management meeting, or they post something on a bulletin board. . . . "

"And some clown writes "NUTS" all over it." I smiled.

"Exactly. Maybe it's a memo to department heads, or a letter. Whatever it is you can be sure that in six months the directive will not be carried out as originally issued or it won't be carried out at all by some departments or some personnel."

"Why?"

"Let's assume the directive is passed out at a management meeting. The president sits behind his oak desk and he says, 'Now, boys, from this day forward I want to get a 2% increase in production from every department every month. Here's how

I want it done: Starting at the end of the month I want a new marketing concept introduced.' Then he spells out his idea on the new concept. That goes on for 15 minutes, then he turns to the production manager, 'As for production, this is what I want to see happen.' Another 15 minutes of explanation. 'And in maintenance, I want inspections done every two weeks, and this is the way a vehicle should be inspected.' And away he goes again."

"I presume they would all have shorthand as one of their management qualifications," I quipped. "But come on, Bob. Presidents don't do those things surely! They would hand out typed instruction sheets." He looked at me quizzically.

"O.K., I'm sorry, I exaggerated," he said. "You're probably right. Let's assume you are right. Out they go with their sheets of paper. What do you think will happen then?"

"Being good managers they will get right to work," I said smiling.

"Providing they have no fires to put out, no problems to clear up, and a whale of a lot of free time on their hands. Agree?"

"Agree, but let's say that's just the way they find things when they get back . . . what's your point?"

"Aha!" he challenged, "how are *they* going to translate this sheet of paper into an action oriented directive?"

"Call a meeting?"

"Probably, how else?"

"Send out a memo to the appropriate people?"

"They will probably do both. Certainly they will study the president's directives to figure out how to implement them, and possibly write up a memo which they can hand out at their first meeting."

"I confess," I said, "That's the way I've done things. What was wrong with it?"

**How the Weekly Management Meeting Can
Become Intensely Productive**

"You tell *me!*" Bob smiled. "Go ahead. Tell me what happened."

"Well, let's see. I remember being on a newspaper's management team. The publisher had a meeting every Tuesday afternoon. On more than one occasion he would finish a casual discussion with a lengthy series of instructions to, say, the production manager or the advertising director."

"What happened?" Bob asked eagerly.

"Well, they would make notes pretty fast . . . "

"Go on, what happened?"

"Well, the next week the boss would ask them what they did about it."

"And what did they tell him?"

"They rarely told him anything. They usually asked him what he was talking about."

Bob threw his head back and laughed! The story tickled him.

"*Perfect!*" he chuckled. "That could not be improved on. That's exactly what *does* happen."

"Not *all* the time, Bob. Sometimes the boss wrote it down for them."

"O.K.," he smiled broadly. "What happened when he did *that?*"

"As I think about it, I can't recall anything happening that made the boss happy. Oh, for awhile things always seemed to improve. Maybe there was more lineage, better layouts, etc. Or maybe the guys quit coming in late in the morning and going home early in the afternoon . . . or stopped taking an hour for coffee . . . or they would send in reports more regularly. But the performance was pretty spasmodic."

"Of *course* it was. It couldn't be any better than spasmodic."

How Operating Letters Force Action

"So how would an O.L. improve it?"

"Essentially in two ways," he replied. "First, the publisher would have laid his instruction down in his Operating Letters. Then it's a directive, it's got a number in the index, it's got a clearly defined position in the binder under a tab marked, say, 'MARKETING.' It will contain the purpose he has in mind in writing this directive. It will spell out exactly *what* he wants done, *how* he wants it done, *who* he wants to do it, and *when* he wants it done. It will state that involved personnel add follow-up P.M.P. and J.P. items. It will be dated for revision and the person revising it—the publisher—or his designate will be named in the Operating Letter."

He was beginning to come through loud and clear.

"Now when the advertising director or the production manager receive their copies," he continued, "*they* can use it as *their* authority for relating to their group exactly what is expected by the publisher. They will probably use the Operating Letter as the basis for one of *their* meetings. If there are specific details to be emphasized they may even have P.M.P. items typed and ready for distribution . . . or J.P. items for their non-management personnel . . . and by doing so they will be locking the accountable functions into a system."

"Would they not write their own O.L. on the subject?" I asked.

"Not too likely. If the publisher's O.L. had been correctly written there wouldn't be any need for them to write an O.L. In fact, as I understand the publisher's position, he would probably have these major department heads read his rough draft before it was finally issued. If any point needed to be clarified, it would have received attention before it came out as an official O.L."

"Wouldn't the O.L. have been read by, say, the salesmen when it was finally issued?" I asked.

"I would certainly think so. An O.L. binder would undoubtedly be located in the department somewhere. Remember, all of the work force should have access to all Operating Letters."

"Then why would the department head have to hold a meeting?"

"Primarily for emphasis. To see that the execution part of the O.L. is carried out . . . that P.M.P. items are written and J.P.'s are prepared."

How to Interrelate Your Responsibilities with Your Subordinate's Accountabilities

"You know, Bob, I'm really beginning to understand what the real difference is between a responsible function and an accountable function. The Operating Letter spells out certain responsibilities for department heads and certain members of the non-management group. But to make people accountable *they* must use P.M.P.'s and J.P.'s. In the case we are talking about, the department head has a responsible function to perform on behalf of the publisher but he also has an accountable function to perform which he delegates to others through P.M.P.'s and J.P.'s . . . but he doesn't lose *control.* So he is responsible and accountable at the same time but he doesn't do all the accountable function himself. He delegates it. But he can also schedule items on his own P.M.P. for personal follow-up as required, right?"

"Good stuff," he said. "You got it a little complicated but I think you've got it. The publisher . . . or the senior manager . . . delegates his own responsibility to the department head. In effect, he is going to hold him responsible for something. But through O.L.'s he is outlining the department head's accountable function as well. You can be sure the department head will be making up P.M.P. items for his own binder and these will remind him of his responsibility to the publisher. However, he delegates the *accountable* function to subordinates. He does it by seeing that the subordinate makes up P.M.P. items, and the non-management people make up J.P.'s. Now he is in that lovely position of having accepted a responsibility from his boss, recorded it in his own P.M.P. binder, and *delegated* the accountable function to others. All bases are covered. The whole thing is locked into the system. No one needs to remember it. They just follow their own P.M.P.'s and their J.P.'s and month after month the correct action is taken."

"From an Operating Letter to a Planned Management Program to a Job Procedure," I reiterated. "Sounds almost like a full circle except I don't see yet how it gets fully rounded out."

"You will," he smiled. "There are two more arcs to the circle and if you're ready we'll start in on the next one."

"I couldn't be more ready, Bob," I said enthusiastically.

EIGHT

How to guarantee
the completion
of every project
you accept
or originate

We had adjourned to the sun deck with our ever-present coffee cups. The give-and-take in our discussions had built a rapport between us and the element of personal friendship was developing fast. In addition to his astuteness as an administrator Bob had a good sense of humor, and as we became more familiar with each other's personalities the conversation became a less stilted question-and-answer interview.

"I think the third phase is a honey," Bob started off as he got comfortable on the upholstered lounge. "It's called the Project Committee System."

To introduce it Bob asked me to go back over my years in business and try to remember the number of times I either launched a project for my work group or participated in a project as an employee, only to have the project disappear into thin air.

"For example," he exclaimed, "have you ever conducted a

management meeting or participated in one in which you or someone else said, 'Whatever happened to that idea so and so came up with regarding such and such?' It may have been a new system, machine, tool, any number of things. And then everybody looks at the ceiling, furrows his brow, and vaguely remembers *something* about it but not enough to offer an opinion."

"Yes," I replied. "It's happened quite a number of times. In fact, I've launched a few for myself that never saw the light of day and I was the only one who was supposed to *do* anything."

"So have I," he continued. "It may be a bit of a stretch but I'd bet a few dollars that 80% of the local managers' projects launched in a company never get finished."

"What happens to them?" I asked.

How Projects Disappear

"Let's ignore the situation where somebody simply forgets to do something. That's the one that causes most of the trouble. But let's say forgetfulness isn't that important." He paused for a second in deep thought. "Here are a few things that can really wreck a good effort. A project is recommended, and feasibility studies are made, a lot of research is done, and just as the project is ready for implementation, perhaps a year after it was suggested, budget priorities change and there's no money. The project is deferred . . . which far too often means it is dead."

"Isn't it?" I asked.

"Well, considering the time and effort that went into it, it shouldn't be."

"Then why is it?"

"Because it is shelved for a future implementation and is *then* forgotten. All the preliminary work is for naught!"

"Won't it be re-introduced when the budget improves?" I asked.

"Yes, if someone remembers to re-introduce it, and I

admit that if it is a major project, like a new building, a new product, etc., it will probably *not* be forgotten. But if it is a minor one, but still one that required a lot of effort, you can be reasonably sure it will be hoisted into never-never land."

How to Overcome Survey Problems and
Save Thousands of Dollars

Bob described a project that originated in the Head Office of a company but involved the branch managers for the research. Senior management wanted to make some major changes in the employees' benefit program.

"It meant that each branch manager had to have a questionnaire completed by every member of his work group. It was done by actually interviewing every member privately. It took about 30 minutes per employee. With a large branch that was a major time investment for the manager. Now there were over 200 branches in this company. You figure out how much time went into the interviewing, the gathering and the analyzing. When it was finished, the company found the bill a little too rich at the time and the project was postponed."

"That seems perfectly reasonable," I said.

"It was," he agreed. "What wasn't reasonable was what happened four years later. Almost the exact same project was *again* launched. I mean another questionnaire was presented. There were a couple of different questions but essentially the objective was the same."

"Maybe they had to update the analysis."

"No way. The questions were not that different. It was still a feasibility study. This was the same project but there was a difference. Know what it was?"

"Nope."

"There was a different vice-president in charge of personnel. He didn't know a project of that exact nature had been launched four years previous."

"Do you think that kind of thing happens regularly?"

"With major projects like that, it doesn't happen, as you say, regularly. But it only has to happen a couple of times and a lot of money, time and energy goes right down the tube."

How to Keep Your Project Committee Meeting on Target

"But it would be different with the small local company, wouldn't it?" I asked.

"Not a bit. In fact, it is even worse. The projects may not be as earth shaking but on a relative basis they are just as prone to premature deaths and just as costly."

"And just as annoying," I added agreeably.

What Happens to Project Assignments

"Right! Did you ever attend a management meeting," he smiled knowingly, "see the boss hand out various project assignments, and watch the guy who gets the assignment try to squirm out of it, offer excuses *right now* why it should be done by someone else or not done at all?"

"I suppose that happens in most management meetings," I said. "I've tried to duck out of a few in my time, I know."

"But usually the boss insists, eh?"

"Usually."

"And when you're chosen as the victim, what do you do? What do the vast majority of victims do?"

"Oh, I suppose they hop right to it, as I did." The tongue was well into my cheek.

"I'll bet," he said derisively. "I'll tell you what most guys do. They make a note of some kind. When they get back to their desks they find the traffic has become badly snarled. There're some phone messages, people waiting to see them, notes are all over their desks. You might say, 'BUSINESS as usual!' Now what happens to the note in the guy's pocket? Know when he finds it? While undressing that night. He empties it with his money, cigarettes, etc., onto the highboy. And when he sees it, he yells 'Sufferin' catfish! I *forgot!*' Then he lies awake all night making sure he won't forget it in the morning. [Short pause.] But what happens when he gets to the office in the morning?"

"He left the note on the highboy?"

"Exactly! But let's assume he didn't *need* the note. He remembered it right up to the very second that he sat down at his desk. Then the traffic started to flow. By ten o'clock he was still remembering it ... vaguely, mind you ... but still it was there and just as soon as he cleared up a couple of things on his desk he'd get right at it. Well, you know how it goes. Then comes next week's management meeting. The boss says, 'Jones, what did you find out about such and such?' "

"And Jones has a case of cardiac arrest!" I chipped in.

"Correct! That project is now hoisted for another week ... at least."

How a Project Committee Is Formed

"O.K., now let me ask you, how does the Project Committee System eliminate the problem?"

"Well, first let's discuss who it is that makes up a Project Committee," he replied. "It is a boss and his immediate subordinates who report directly to him. No one else. As you go down through the management levels each manager would have a Project Committee, again consisting of himself and his immediate subordinates. Now this usually stops at the level of the first line management group. In other words, non-management personnel rarely serve on a Project Committee unless they are specifically brought in to contribute some particular expertise they may have that might be needed in a certain project. But this would be temporary. For one project only, so to speak."

"Good heavens!" I interjected, "isn't that a lot of committees? Wouldn't that produce a paper storm in handling the minutes, the reports, etc.?"

"Negative," he replied. "The paper work is nothing. There are no minutes and the only reports that are ever written are the ones that describe the finished product, or, if approved by management, the directive that puts the project into motion . . . usually an Operating Letter."

"But in the case of a large company," I insisted, "that would mean a lot of committees, a lot of time lost, a lot of schedule interruptions."

"Nonsense, Gordon," he said somewhat disgusted. "Meetings are being held every week by most managers right now. The trouble with them is they are gab fests, bitch sessions. They aren't planned that way but they usually wind up that way. And as for minutes, reports, etc., they do, at the present time and with most companies, consume hours of time to be written up, discussed and voted on. This does not happen in a Project Committee meeting."

"If you have five levels of management in a company would you have five Project Committees?" I asked.

"Not necessarily. Four would be the correct number although even that depends on the attitude of the senior manager."

"What does that mean?" I asked.

"Well, he might not feel that more than one Project Committee is justified. In a small company it probably isn't. In one with five levels of management, I would certainly encourage four committees, but that is a local decision."

How to Get Vertical Cooperation Between One Project Committee and Another

"Bob," I said, "even though it's discretionary, your own recommendation still sounds like a lot of committees. What's to stop them from all doing the same project?"

"Essentially the system," he replied. "A project, launched we'll say by the senior manager's P.C. group, will usually involve management at lower levels. That means a district manager working on a division manager's P.C. would probably have numerous things to check out to fill the assignment he got from his boss at a P.C. meeting. He may delegate parts of the assignment to some members of his own P.C. group. By this kind of communication, people down the line tend to be informed on what is going on."

"All well and good!" I said, "as long as the project is coming down the pike. But what happens when a district manager's committee takes on a project? Does the division manager know what's going on?"

"If the project is significant enough for it to be acted on by the division manager's committee, the project will probably be sent right to that committee. But if it's strictly a district project, he won't know about it until he does an inspection . . . the last part of the whole 4BMAP System."

How to Capture the Creative Input of Managers

"Has the district manager the authority to act on a project without the division manager knowing anything about it?" I felt a little naive when I asked the question . . . more so when I got the answer.

"Of course he has. What do you think he's paid for! If the project is too extensive he'll be the first one to know it and it will be put on the division manager's desk right away. But there are dozens of projects that district or sub-managers can take on to improve things in their own jurisdiction. They don't need authority. They've got it by virtue of their appointment."

I was still mentally wrestling with the number of committees this system seemed to be creating. When four out of five levels of management have project committees, all I could think about was time invested in a committee room. It was incorrect thinking, as it turned out, but I wanted to get it clarified so I went back to it.

"Bob, it still sounds like a lot of new committees for a company—a large investment of management time and effort."

"As we are talking about it, it does. In practice, however, it simply harnesses the creative effort that is—or should be—going on all the time. Management needs the creative

assistance of its subordinate managers. Those who serve on
P.C.'s are junior managers . . . usually competent, imaginative,
and leaders. These are the people management calls on now.
The only difference is that instead of casual, unorganized,
frequent meetings and discussions, under the P.C. system the
discussions are organized, methods are known, procedures
understood. It's nothing at all for a Project Committee to deal
with 15 to 25 projects in a one-hour meeting, and not one piece
of paper comes out of the meeting. Only one-sentence notes are
made on each project by each committee member since they all
have copies of each project.

"Once there is acceptance of a project," he continued,
"there is no way for it to get out of the system until it is
completed or until the committee intentionally abandons it."

"If 4BMAP was installed in a company," I asked, "would
it be mandatory for each level of management to have a Project
Committee?"

"Of course not!" he replied emphatically. "I've already
said that management is in complete control. They may want to
confine P.C. activities to senior executives only, and that's their
privilege.

"But let me say this," he went on. "One of the greatest
sources of ideas is management resource. If it is used to wrestle
with a problem, the answer to it is likely to come out ten times
faster than if senior management alone did all the thinking.

How Participatory Management Can Stop
Grievances Before They Arise

"What most top level managers are afraid of is revealing to
their subordinates their own inability to solve a problem. The
consequence is 'Keep the problem to myself'—or, 'Maybe it will
go away'—or, 'I hope someone else comes up with an answer.'

"By this means the answers are at best delayed unneces-
sarily, at worst never discovered at all." He paused to let that
sink in, then, "what I'm saying is the P.C. system is a
management system. The managers are expected to introduce

problems that need answers ... or projects that need exploration. They *know* that is the name of the game. No one suffers any loss of prestige. Their self-image is protected. The senior boss ... the chairman of the committee ... is in complete control because this system is part of *his* management technique.

"On the other hand the members of the committee—his subordinate managers—participate. They enjoy it! They are involved. And when projects are implemented they see that the implementation goes smoothly." He turned to look me square in the eye and said, "with these potential rewards, why not have P.C.'s at each level of management?" He pointed his finger at himself. "Look," he went on, "I'm a division manager. I have my project committee. The members are made up of the immediate subordinates who report to me. Each D.M. has a project committee. The members are his immediate subordinates. Now not all supervisors have committees but many of them do. That's their privilege. I don't force them.

"Suppose a supervisor's committee comes up with a project which goes beyond its administrative or authoritative powers; it sends the project to the next level. It may be killed there or that level may take it on—*or* send it to still the next level. In any event, the project is dealt with and the originating committee is informed. Nothing gets lost and every project is acted upon. When management assignments change you never lose a project because the replacement is automatically assigned the project so it continues to completion."

How the System Pays Off

"This may sound fatuous," I said, "but has it really paid off?"

"A rather foolish question," he smiled. (Long pause.) "Look, my division is probably the best division in the system. I'll get hell from my colleagues for that, but it is. Know why? Because we have a bunch of guys working on projects. We don't live with a problem five minutes. As soon as any level of management identifies a problem, we're after the solution! The one that finds it is either going to solve it or know exactly what to do to get it to a higher level *for* solution.

"And here's another thing. Guess what this can do for morale! The finest way to kill incentive, destroy initiative, etc., is to ignore the creative potential of people, or to deny them an organized system by which their creativeness can be tapped, their expertise displayed and their interest appreciated. And there are hundreds ... thousands ... of companies who are doing this. Furthermore, labor is taking full advantage of them."

"Then why," I asked, "does labor continue to go for more wages? Why don't they go for systems like yours? As I see this phase of the system, it sounds like the grand beginning of participatory management."

"You're right, and I'll have more to say about that in a few minutes! As for labor going for wages, that's only what the public hears and reads. Negotiations today are *not* just for wages. In the last five to ten years there has been a substantial change in the direction of labor demands, and every time I think about it I'm struck with the relationship between what they are asking for and what would normally and properly come before a Project Committee."

"Isn't there a chance of the Project Committee becoming essentially a bargaining committee?" I interrupted.

"Not a chance in the world!" he said emphatically. "The Project Committees are composed of *management* personnel. However, let me emphasize this: as a result of Project Committee activity, many items that *would* represent grievances are brought to light and usually resolved long before they land on a bargaining desk."

"Then how come you have strikes?" I asked rather sarcastically.

"How come I have strikes? Well, I'll tell you. We are just a small part of the whole system. When the system goes on strike we go right along with it. Now I'm not going to be quoted as saying my work group would *not* strike if they had the privilege. The thing is, they don't have the privilege to make the final decision on a strike so the question is purely academic.

Knowing What Workers Want

"What I want to get across is this," he stressed. "Through a Project Committee System you should *know* what is wanted. You can, from that position, effectively deal with the things wanted whatever way it's possible for you to deal with them. You don't have to sit back and wait for the day of bargaining and have it all dropped on you like a ton of bricks.

"Again, don't misunderstand or misquote me. No Project Committee can *solve* every demand that comes to it any more than you can *implement* all of them, and when you can't, it's the job of a manager to explain *why* you can't. If the explanation isn't accepted then you might be surprised at how often you might be staring that issue down at the bargaining table. But you would also be surprised at how often an explanation is accepted. The work force are not stupid. They listen with reason to any explanation that is itself reasonable.

"Certainly there are rabble-rousers in every union—guys that just like to keep things churned up. I won't talk about their motives, but I believe they are less motivated to the real needs of the worker than they would have you believe. However, union *members,* as distinct from union *leaders,* will always be more reasonable if they know they have an outlet for some positive action on their requests. Many non-management people have good ideas and they pass these along to their bosses who evaluate them and usually assign them as projects for a Project Committee to follow up."

"The Project Committee System has no union aspects at all then but in effect *does* solve problems before they become union problems. Is that right?"

"That's right. We don't relate the P.C. System to unions; it has nothing directly to do with unions. P.C.'s are *management* groups, but as managers they automatically have work force problems as one important consideration. What's good for the work force isn't *always* good for the company, but it happens. Any time production quotas, quality standards, etc., do not depend on the *work force,* look for the big cheese moon in the sky. They directly depend on them, so the 'people' situation is, and should be, uppermost in the minds of management.

"Again, the P.C. System is the device, the means by which projects see the light of day, get locked into the system, are *never* lost or forgotten, and *always* see completion—even if completion means abandonment. The thing is, management is in control of the final decision and it must make a final decision. Projects cannot just peter out or be ignored. If the committee accepts the project, it *must* go to completion. Curtailed budgets, transfer of personnel, resignations, etc., have no affect on the completion factor. The project *must* be completed or be intentionally abandoned or postponed. And the system makes sure that's what happens!"

"O.K., Bob," I said, "just for a moment let's go to, say, a district manager's committee. What kind of projects would you expect it to take on?"

"There's a little point right there. I don't *expect* it to take on any project. It takes on projects it *wants* to take on and there is no limit. If it spots a bottleneck or a roadblock in the production sequence it will go right after it. If there's a faulty communication line to the work group, it will work on that, or fix a safety problem, or any number of things.

"I can think of a project involving storage space in the trucks. Racks and shelves were not adequate. The project was taken on and a complete redesigning job was done on the interior of the trucks. The result was an increase in productivity and a much happier work group."

How a Manager's Project Committee Can
Improve the Working Conditions of an
Entire Work Group

He poured another cup of coffee and sat silent for a minute. Then, "I get a feeling," he said, "that you would like to see the P.C. System as something to do with labor/management relations. Am I right?"

"Well, if it adds a single positive dimension to the issue of labor/management, I would *certainly* like to see it."

"Indeed it does, but I would have to put it all in the category of prevention more than intention. I mean by that, there was not, nor will there ever be, an intention to make 4BMAP a labor/management tool. Where it might appear to be a tool is coincidental, and it is best reflected in the word *prevention*—often accidental prevention!"

How Project Committees Can Improve Working Conditions

"What does that mean?" I asked.

"Simply this: the Project Committees are often dealing with methods to improve productivity, increase efficiency, reduce costs, improve sales and safety, and so forth. A byproduct of these projects often involves improvements for the entire work force. Many of them directly relate to working conditions and therefore relate to people at the job stations. It's obvious that if a project improves things, the people involved are going to share in the improvement."

"I'm not sure I get your point where it relates to labor-management relations," I interrupted.

"Well, my point is this. If you have active Project Committees, very few annoyances get past you. If an annoyance of some kind is causing bottlenecks or roadblocks, your attention as a manager is drawn to it because of the decrease in production. Instead of living with the situation you get it into a Project Committee. When the committee has done its job, you will make changes to get rid of the roadblock, and many times those changes directly affect people. So, in respect to the labor/management situation you have probably prevented a grievance from even being expressed."

"And that's what you call accidental prevention," I said.

"Accidental only insofar as what came out is a solution to a 'down' situation in the production processes," he explained.

"In other words, if there hadn't been a bottleneck in the first place, the thing that might have wound up as a grievance is not likely to have been noticed?"

"Unless it was quite obvious," he answered. "But here again, those things that are obviously potential grievances, not involving salary, overtime, or fringe benefits, are *likely* to be on a Project Committee's agenda. In short, because there is a Project Committee, management has a place to handle issues long before they get to be serious grievances."

"Would you say that it boils down to 'anything goes' for a Project Committee?" I suggested.

"Not anything," he cautioned. "It has its boundaries. But anything that affects job stations will be examined and if it is outside the committee's jurisdiction it will be referred to the Project Committee that *has* the authority to deal with it. Don't forget, in industry as a whole, only about 20% of the local manager's projects ever get completed. With the P.C. System, 100% of the projects are completed or abandoned on purpose."

"In a smaller company would this not replace many of the management meetings it is prone to have?" I asked.

How to Handle Fifteen Projects in an Hour!

"Good point. A Project Committee will do *just* that. It can turn what is often a gab fest into an action packed meeting. As I've said, most P.C.'s will actually discuss 15 or more projects in a one-hour meeting."

"Would they really be giving proper attention to the projects?" I queried.

"Yes, all that a project needs. When one is accepted it is assigned to one man who acts as project chairman. From then on he is working to a laid-on target date. Each meeting requires him to tell the committee only what his final action to date has been. For example, say a project to install overhead lights in one section of an assembly line is taken on by a committee. A project chairman is appointed and a target date selected, possibly a month from then. They hold meetings once a week. All that project chairman would report would be the last most important thing he had done. His report might be one sentence: 'Prices for the lights now being obtained.' Each member would write that report onto his copy of the project status report. That's all the notes they ever take."

"Oh, each member has a copy of the project status report?"

"Yes, all members receive a typewritten copy of the project at the time it is introduced. From then on each member writes in the current information at each meeting. They put each project in their P.C. binder which they bring to every meeting. They make running notes on the status report so they can see at a glance exactly what is happening to every project. When a project is completed, the status report is filed into the completed section of their binder. In this way they keep a current project right before them but can make instant reference to those that are completed."

How to Avoid Launching a Project for the Second Time

"Is there any special reason why the ones completed are kept?" I asked.

"One reason is to make sure they don't launch the same project twice."

"How could that ever happen?"

"Very easily. Let's say there is a project that simply couldn't be completed. The final decision was abandonment. Before that decision was made a lot of work could have gone into it. Then a year later we have new men on the committee, or a new chairman, and in comes the same project. And the work is started all over."

"Well, other things may have changed too. Maybe the project could be completed this time," I remarked.

"Agreed! But having the running report on the previous

effort will soon establish what 'condition' has changed that may make the project feasible. Without the report they go through the same exercise all over again. With the running notes they may actually save themselves dozens of steps or not start it at all because nothing has happened or changed enough to justify their taking it on again."

How to Keep Committee Effectiveness High

"What happens if a man who has been assigned a couple of projects leaves?" I asked.

"He is replaced and his P.C. binder is transferred to the new man. The replacement usually takes over unfinished projects and is clued in on them by the incumbent and by the notes on the project status report," he assured.

"Then that's why projects are never lost just because a man is, right?"

"Right!" he answered.

How the Status Report Eliminates Minutes

"Let's talk about the status reports," I said, picking up a sample. "It seems to me that while these one-sentence reports sure cut down on the talking in a committee meeting and are a vast improvement over the long written minutes, are one-sentence efforts sufficient as a usable running history?"

"Good point, and they are," he replied. "But the project chairman would probably keep more extensive notes on his copy. He may even build a project file. However, his report to the committee is simply a progress report. That's why it is called a Project Status Report. The rest of the group should be interested only in the last most important thing done on the project prior to the meeting."

He rummaged in his briefcase but couldn't find what he was looking for. "Darn it," he said, "I thought I had a good example of the typical kind of minutes that are usually taken at management meetings. I got it from one of the students. It was a dilly! Started off with 'The meeting was called to order by so and so,' and it went on and on about someone moving that such and such happen—seconded by so and so—passed by a majority, etc. etc. Without a doubt the man who wrote those minutes probably lost two hours doing them and I wouldn't be surprised if they had been read and edited a couple of times by others before they were finally typed.

"I know of companies where they couldn't hold a meeting because the minutes of the previous meeting hadn't been typed. Talk about the wheels of progress grinding to a halt!" he gasped.

How to Keep Speeches Out of the Committee Room

"And then you get to the meetings themselves," he said. "Many of them are just opportunities for speeches. They spend hours in prittle-prattle!"

"In other words, a Progress Committee meeting wants status only and not all the verbiage that explains how it got to that status?" I questioned.

"Exactly. What's the good of the verbiage? It just uses up time. Its *only* possible advantage is to give the project chairman an opportunity to make speeches on how great he is! The committee isn't interested. His greatness lies in the completion process, not in the doing process."

"Well, suppose he wants the advice of the committee and/or the P.C. chairman himself?"

"Then he comes to the meeting with questions and he asks them," said Bob.

"Suppose he wants some assistance; can he call on members of the committee?" I asked.

"He can if he wants. However, as project chairman he should have access to others on his working team at his job station who can be called upon. Every member of the Project Committee is a manager so it becomes his responsibility to harness his own resources to complete the projects. In some cases he will use personnel from other work groups."

"Now I'm beginning to see why a Project Committee can bounce around 20 or more projects at the same time. Most committees in companies keep all the action in the committee," I said.

"Dead on. In most companies, when 4BMAP isn't controlling the process, a project is accepted and then the chairman starts handing out parts of the project to various members. In about three projects every man in the room is assigned something to do and until those projects are completed, no more projects are undertaken," he explained. "And at subsequent meetings you would have four or five guys reporting on one single project. It's foolish to use up the time of the real organizers in the company by getting them busy doing a small segment of a single project. Instead of the members harnessing others to carry out the effort, they do it themselves.

"And because they do, they can't handle more than one or two projects at a time. Listen, my project team, right now, have 57 projects in motion! We have completed 14, so that leaves 43—and we'll discuss all 43 in a two-hour meeting."

How to Get Your Employee Group to Agree to Change

"In effect, then," I interjected, "the project chairman, as distinct from the committee chairman, would be building under him a working team composed of men and women who are not actually on the project committee, although some could be members of other project committees? Right?"

"In most cases, and probably different men and women for different projects. I'm sure you can see what this does."

"It makes a lot of people get involved," I offered.

"It sure does. And when people participate they get interested and when they are interested they are usually a whale of a lot happier and more productive."

"And one more thing," I said excitedly. "They accept change a whole lot better."

"How right you are! There is nothing more difficult to do

than to get people to accept change. I think more things are *not* done that *should* be done for this simple reason than anything I can think of. I've seen extremely good ideas lie on the planning board simply because resistance to change would make it too difficult to implement them."

"Even those changes that are imposed can fail," I added. "In fact, I suppose it is an experience like that in a company that makes an executive reluctant to try new ideas. He gets a little gun shy, wouldn't you think?"

"He sure does. There are thousands of executives whose careers have been negatively affected *not* because of their ideas but because their ideas just never worked. They couldn't get the work force to accept them, and naturally they are judged on *implementation*, not on the idea," Bob answered.

"Would you say the P.C. System would eliminate this kind of resistance?" I asked.

"Well, 'eliminate' may be a bit exaggerated. It would sure cut it down, and assuming you have the right managers on the committee it would *eventually* eliminate it."

"What do you mean by 'the right managers'?"

"The kind of man who can get other people to do what he wants them to do and like it. That's considered the best definition of 'selling' there is, and unless a manager is a good salesman he's not likely to be a good manager."

"And naturally," I added, "that begins with selling his chosen few to help him do the exploration work on the project he is assigned. And I suppose as he gets involved in the exploration phase he gets others interested and involved."

"That's for sure. By the time the project is researched and implementation begins you've got a dozen or so people sold on it. It makes implementation fairly easy. People will always work harder for something they had a part in creating in the first place. It's like parenthood. Let them have a few of the labor pains and they see that the offspring stays healthy!"

"Good analogy," I smiled. "Is there anything else about the Project Committee System that you would like to add?"

"Well, of course there's a lot we haven't talked about, such as indexing, controlling, handling the meeting and so forth. But I think you've got the major points covered. The thing that is really important with the P.C. System is the way it can effectively handle numerous projects at the same time without one of them ever getting lost. Once the project is accepted, the system prevents it from disappearing into thin air even when personnel change or budgets are restricted, or the general climate isn't right. The accepted project *must* be a completed project, even if completion means a decision to abandon it. That decision *must* be made and recorded."

"And if I could complete the summation," I added, "the P.C. System has *not,* I concede, anything to do with union participation!" We both laughed!

How Bob Takes Formal Education Apart
and Puts It Back Together

"You're sure you're not just saying that," Bob chided.

"No, I'm not. I admit it is about a 180° turn from my original position, but I have a feeling that, as with the other two parts of this 4BMAP System, there are some subtleties that are difficult to spot the first time around."

"There most certainly are," Bob agreed. "I think you could write a book on subtleties and never mind the system! Every damn manager in this country wants to be effective! The vast majority are trained to be effective, one way or another. You know, they go to a university, take courses, attend seminars, read trade magazines and papers and books until they're bug-eyed. They become theoreticians, strategists, analysts, statisticians and technicians . . . and *still* fail. It's a helluva shame, a major indictment against the whole educational process. You shouldn't encourage me. I get so hot when I think of the money and time that is spent on management training which, in actual practice, hardly sees the light of day, I boil over! I'll tell you how hot I am. I wouldn't let a single member of my work group take a course . . . other than a trades skill course . . . who wasn't working with the 4BMAP System. I wouldn't waste his time or his company's money. If he hadn't a *system* to put into practice what he *learned* in the course, he'd never see the inside of the classroom."

"Boy, you're making it pretty tough for the educationists we've got," I said.

"And well I should! If they educate without having as their final objective a means by which their students can *implement* what they have taught them, they should be indicted for incompetence!"

"I know this is a pet of yours, but are you suggesting that a degree in commerce or, say, a Master's in Business Administration is useless?" I challenged.

How Systems Make Knowledge Operative

"Why do you have to go to extremes?" he asked. "No, of course I'm not saying it's useless. If you don't have theory, strategy, marketing knowledge, etc., the best system in the world will be no good to you because you won't have anything to put into it. I'm just saying it works the other way, too. While we have much going for us in the *knowledge* department, we have very damn little going for us in the *system* department."

"Take Management by Objectives. I've mentioned it before," I said trying to get him down to actual cases. "That's a pretty good theory and much has been written about it. Are you really suggesting it's useless without a system to implement it?"

"I'm suggesting *exactly* that," he said with finality! "The *concept* of M.B.O. is just great, but for every executive who understands the concept I'll point out three who haven't a clue on how to make it operative." He paused, then, "We talked about P.P.B.S. too, remember?" [Programmed Planning Budget Systems.]

"Yes, I do."

"What do you really know about it?" he asked.

"I think I read something about it in some educational magazine," I replied.

"That's probably where you heard about it all right," he said. "It *is* primarily within the educational system that it's having quite a play.

"May I say right off the bat, it makes sense. It's a well-thought-out system. School districts are well advised to study at least parts of it. But let me also say that without a system like 4BMAP to *implement* P.P.B.S. there is hardly a chance that it won't bog down in a morass of confusion. In fact, it could drive an administrator out of his tree and make the guy who tried to implement it look so foolish it could mean the end of his career."

The Difficulty of Implementing

"Well, why is it so difficult to implement?" I asked.

"Simply because the system has no vehicle by which it can be carried into an organization," he replied.

"Isn't it its own vehicle?" I suggested.

"It's supposed to be, and if everyone could remember exactly how to communicate to each other about the system, exactly who does what, when, and how he does it, and no one is transferred, it *would* work," he answered.

"Well, isn't it mapped out for the originator? It seems to me I saw a diagram of the system. It covered those points," I observed.

"Undoubtedly you've seen a diagram but it sure didn't cover those points ... even if it said that here the superintendent does this and that, and then the principal of the school does this and so forth. Telling them what to do is not guaranteeing it will continue to be done or that they will do it *as it is supposed to be done.* And it does not guarantee that the subordinate work force will do it or continue to do it, or guarantee the introduction of forms to do it, or the acceptance of the system at *any* level ... including the superintendent himself!"

"Doesn't it start with the superintendent?" I asked.

"It may, but it's more likely to be a trustee who brings it

up at a school district board meeting. The superintendent may be assigned to explore it, but whether he does it or not is another thing. And whether he will see its value considering the time and cost of installation is still another. But worst of all by far is the danger of its being accepted without having the sub-system to guarantee its installation."

"And that, of course, is where 4BMAP comes in," I chided.

"Naturally!" he sighed, "that's where 4BMAP comes in!"

"You know, Bob," I said, "as I talk to you I'm suddenly confronted with the feeling that we tend to succeed in business more by accident than by intention! I get a feeling that we are playing a big game called 'Throw Mud at the Fence.' Some of it is bound to stick but a whale of a lot of it falls off. In other words, we have enough technical and administrative knowledge within industry to muddy up the fence pretty good, but if we had a means of putting more 'stickum' in the mud balls, our aim would be better and many more of the balls would stay put."

"I couldn't have said it better," he laughed. "If the mud is knowledge, then the 'stickum' is system! Put them together and you just have to hit more bull's-eyes!"

NINE

How the detailed job inspection system puts it all together

At about the time we completed our discussion of the P.C phase, Mrs. Babbidge had completed her tasks in the kitchen.

"If you boys want a cocktail before supper, you had better have it now," she said. "I'll give you exactly half an hour and then this supper goes . . . hot or cold."

"Gee, you're sure tough on a guy," Bob teased. "It will take us half an hour just to finish the P.C. phase."

"It had better not because there will be no 'happy hour' for either of you if it does. So get with the Johnny Walker if you're going to."

Bob poured, and as we enjoyed the less intense rays of the sinking sun he continued to vent his feelings about the general inadequacies of the educational process as it related to the development of administrative expertise. He made a point of avoiding trade skill or professional technique training, certain elements of sales and marketing training ("but 4BMAP has just as important a function to fulfill in a company's marketing department as it has in its administrative departments"), and he eliminated such procedures as accounting ("a trial balance is a trial balance and if you have training as an accountant you know how to strike one off") and actuarial procedures in a life insurance company, and such other highly organized technical skills which by the very nature of the practitioner's training he knew what to do, how to do it, when and why.

But short of these, and as supplementary assists to these, he felt that knowledge had to go hand in hand with a system to apply it, and that few universities seemed to be cognizant of the need for a practical system by which students could take out of the halls of learning everything that they could remember and apply it on a job station.

How the 4BMAP System Can Reduce
Executive Turnover

"Management," he said earnestly, "looks to the university graduate as the base for its long range executive needs. It hires him because he is supposed to have learned a lot more than, say, the high school graduate. He has demonstrated initiative, resourcefulness, etc. But when management has no system by which that graduate can apply his knowledge, it might just as well hire a high school student and train him from scratch. In fact, the company would probably have a more contented employee. The university graduate who can't unleash his expertise becomes a highly frustrated individual before very long. He'll move . . . and believe me, many are moving. The wandering executive is usually a university graduate, and while there are dozens of reasons for the movements, one of them is usually described as 'inadequate opportunity.' Whenever I hear that, I ask myself, opportunity? or system? Nine times out of ten it will be system! The graduate himself doesn't know the system and the company doesn't have one. So the poor guy jumps from position to position, wondering all the time what's wrong with management and management wondering what's wrong with him. With hardly an exception it could be stopped if there was just some system by which the man's full knowledge could be applied and the company's full potential reached."

How the 4BMAP System Can Provide a Valuable
Tool for Self-Actualization

I thought for a moment. Bob was onto something fairly significant. "I mentioned subtleties in the 4BMAP system," I said. "I suppose you have just mentioned one when you talk about executive movement and one reason for it. I can think of quite a few others."

"Be my guest," he said with anticipation.

"Well, I can see where this system has quite a potential with one of my own pet theories . . . aided and abetted of course by people like Douglas McGregor and his Theory X and Theory Y, as well as Abe Maslow and his Theory of Motivation."

"I'm listening," he said putting his glass on the sun deck. "I think I know what you're going to say and you will be one of the first observers of this system to say it. So fire away!"

"Possibly it's not as profound as you may think, but it's important. As you know, it was McGregor who hypothesized that the traditional management concept . . . his Theory X . . . was that people had to be driven to make them work, that they disliked work, were almot incapable of self-control and therefore had to be supervised at all times. The main motivation force used was 'a carrot as a bribe and a stick as a threat.' That's not new to you.

"And as you know, his Theory Y went in opposite directions. It presumed that within the make-up of a man there was a great desire to feel important, to gain recognition, to be in on things, to have his opinions sought out and his suggestions respected. This approach, according to the theory, would bring about employee participation, give him substantial job satisfaction and thereby improve his morale and expand his cooperative concepts . . . make him more willing to cooperate with management and with his co-workers."

"Excuse the interruption," Bob interjected. "But when you hear about the Detailed Job Inspection System, you're going to flip. Go ahead, I'm with you 100%."

**The Five Basic Needs Every Manager
Should Understand**

"O.K. Then we have Maslow and his theory on motivation . . . and *this* expert I really dig! Maslow's contribution to management was to point out in simple language just what man's motivation needs were. He said there were five basic needs:

1. Physiological needs . . . the lowest form, basic to everyone, involving essentially food, clothing and shelter, with a little sleep.
2. Safety needs . . . the desire for protection from danger or the threat of danger to himself or his family or his source of the first need . . . like the company that pays the rent.
3. The need to belong . . . this has to do with a man's relationship with others in his environment, his place in the social group and sub-elements of the whole group. I mean, he may have a need to belong to the Rotary Club and just as strong a need to belong to one of the committees within the club.
4. Esteem needs . . . these are interrelated to the third need. If he 'belongs' he is somewhat satisfying his esteem needs. But it goes further. Esteem means *self*-esteem, self-respect. He needs to know he is achieving something that he enjoys, has self-confidence, is sufficiently independent so as to be able to use his own resources to complete the achievement. Then, of course it also involves the esteem of others in his peer group and those who appear to be his superiors. This

takes in such things as his reputation, his status, his importance, and the appreciation expressed to him for his contribution.

5. Finally, the need for self-actualization. This one has been overlooked the most by both union and management and it's the one that has been hitting me time after time today as we have been discussing 4BMAP. This is the intense desire we all have for self-fulfillment, to fully utilize the talents we inherited or acquired, to become whatever we are capable of becoming without being short-changed by either our own mental fears or imposed limitations or by actions, unawareness, ignorance or indifference of others . . .like managers, for instance!

"Now, when you put these needs under the microscope of management effectiveness," I went on, "you find that management has done a reasonably good job in satisfying the first one. The physiological needs are reasonably well satisfied even if the unions have to get the credit for the satisfaction. But having said that, let me also say that union leadership is still flogging away at the first need. They're still pursuing the buck—the wage increase—as the prime focal point for their attack . . . "

"Oh, I can't entirely agree with you there, Gordon," Bob interrupted. "As I have already said, they get that reputation because the media gives it to them. You should sit in at a bargaining session. It certainly includes wages, but it sure as heck includes a lot of other things that the media just don't bother printing because they know very well what constitutes sensationalism . . . what catches the reader's eye. I mean, a headline that screams, 'TWENTY PERCENT WAGE BOOST TO ELECTRICAL WORKERS,' is going to sell a lot more newspapers than one that says, 'Labor Wants Safety Goggles.' "

"You didn't let me finish," I bounced back, "Although you have made the point very well, I said wages were their prime focal point of attack, but they have moved to the second need—the safety needs—and have moved to them aggressively.

The business of tenure is a safety need . . . safe from dismissal, layoffs, etc.—which, as I indicated, has an interrelationship with the first need, the physiological need. And of course, the whole field of safety is part of their bargaining platform."

"And it has been ever since old man Lewis raised Cain about safety conditions in the mines," Bob emphasized.

How Management Has Permitted the Worker to Switch His Allegiance

"Agreed. It's not a new approach, but when we get to the third need, the need to belong, what do we see? That need is much more fulfilled by unions than by management. The worker doesn't belong to management. He belongs to the union. Management has not found the way in which he can embrace the man as part of the whole force that makes the company successful. Oh, they give lip service to it, but they simply do not have a system by which workers are intentionally interwoven into the fabric of management. Management *wants* to embrace them. I think they know that they *need* to embrace them but they certainly don't seem to know *how* to do it. They may have their grievance committees . . . I do hate that title . . . or they have suggestion boxes . . . complaint memos . . . bitch sessions on a one-to-one basis, and with a few brave managers, on a group basis.

"But," I continued, "it all comes out smelling like condescension. Like management was saying, 'Labor, you're Peck's bad boy but we need you so we'll let you squeak out a suggestion once in awhile and give you a chance to blow off some steam occasionally and that should satisfy you! Now get back to the oars or we'll slap your wrist!' "

I went on to say that I didn't honestly think management wanted to be this way. Perhaps in the past, but certainly not now. But it didn't know how to get with it. "It's like the bashful kid at the dance. He wants to ask Susie for a dance but he doesn't know how to do it so he stands on the sidelines and watches Susie get the rush from the big redheaded oaf who isn't going to be satisfied with just a dance, he wants to kiss her and seduce her too!"

Bob was laughing uproariously. I didn't think it was that funny. As I looked behind me I realized he didn't really think so either . . . Mrs. Babbidge was standing in the doorway. "I think I'm missing something," she laughed. "Who's getting seduced around here? Who's Susie and what company does she work with?"

Well, that broke up the serious discussion. When we stopped laughing, Mrs. Babbidge said, "I just came out to tell you supper is served. I didn't think you had got around to sex already."

The three of us had an almost burlesque supper. One joke lead to another and when they ran out we went into puns and limericks. I can't remember when I felt so comfortable, welcome and relaxed. These were truly wonderful people. They had an intense interest in life and living. As a team they were unmatched by most couples of my acquaintance. Joyce's interest in Bob was not a clinging, superficially lavish panto-mime. It was genuine, amazingly informed and articulate. She had been over the bumps with Bob all the way and while her home was the very epitome of luxurious grace, her behavior was without affectation or sham. No airs were put on and many references to the 'good ole days' clearly revealed a determined struggle to raise standards, leave behind the lunch-bucket, and through intelligent attention to growth and development take a place in society that would be the envy of millions.

The meal was truly epicurean, crowned with a choice of dessert. But that's not the amazing item! Bob has one eating eccentricity. To my shuddering amazement he had chocolate cake liberally spread with peanut butter covered with a huge helping of ice cream! A liqueur followed the dessert and that was followed by coffee on the sun deck.

By this time the sun was struggling to chin itself on the horizon. The air was still warm but as we sat down on the lounges, Joyce brought out sweaters. "If I know my Bob, he'd sooner shiver than interrupt a conversation to come in and get this. I'll be back for you boys at nine, and no later."

"I'm almost sorry we had to eat," Bob said. "But I know exactly where we stopped. You were talking about the big redheaded lout giving a bad time to Susie!" We both chuckled again.

"Yes, Susie. Well of course, as you know, Susie is the worker and the big lout is labor and the bashful kid is management. And it's management that doesn't know how to get Susie to dance. And as I've said before while seeing this system today, I'm beginning to think that you have at long last put the words (the system) into management's hands and pretty soon there's going to be lyrics and a lot of "Waltz Me Matilda" going on in industry!"

"I think you're right, Gordon," Bob agreed with a broad grin straining at his ear lobes. "While we may sound like braggards, Dr. Dacus and I are kinda proud of it. But go on with your theories about motivation. I'm really interested."

"Well, I think I dealt with the third need, the need to belong. As I said, the rank and file belong to labor more than to management and until this changes they will always incline themselves in that direction.

How Participatory Management Is Often Killed by Those Who Want It

"The fourth need gets a little sticky . . . the esteem need! It gets sticky because management is somewhat frightened about giving a man an opportunity to flex his own muscles. Here again, it wants the guy to have self-esteem, self-confidence, a sense of independence that permits him to use his own resources, but it is more or less afraid that he will kick over the traces, usurp the management function or prerogative and start telling management what to do instead of vice versa."

Bob was very contemplative for a moment and then he jumped right in with, "And because of this fear it holds him down. *But,* it doesn't *want* to hold him down. It *knows* he can offer a whale of a lot to the job station, both in the way of doing the job well and in the way of finding better ways to do it. But because . . . and this is the point . . . because there is no controlled system it can't let the full concept of participatory management loose. It is afraid it will run away with the shop. No brakes. Why not admit it, *you* had the same fear. Now I know what you meant when you showed concern about the labor/management thing. With 4BMAP you *can* get involved with participatory management and *not* get the backlash of over-indulgence in the management function."

"Exactly," I agreed. "That's why I get a little excited about *your* system. It has these subtleties. I'm not sure you are really aware of them yourself."

"Oh, you'd better believe I'm aware of them! I may not be as involved in them as you are . . . from a professional point of view . . . but I sure know they are there simply because I know that when a company or an organization installs the system, they find too many things going *right* for them. What I mean is, the system looks after most of the things you are talking about even though they were not the things that motivated Pence Dacus and me to develop it."

"It's quite amazing how it all fits," I said as I contemplated just what their original motive was and what the system was doing without its authors really knowing what it could or would do. I felt I was talking to a man who had found a cure for the common cold but found after he did so that he had just discovered a cure for T.B.!

Why Job Station Creativeness Depends on a System as Much as on Talent

"Well, let me go on," I said. "You may break your arm patting your own back but do you see how 4BMAP can provide the fifth need . . . the need for self-actualization as Maslow says?"

"I think I can but you tell me, I'm modest," he coaxed, grinning.

"Well, you've been preaching it all day. 'It gives the manager a chance to think and plan, to create and innovate'—

those were the words I think you used. It boils down to giving the manager a chance to fully utilize his competence ... to self-actualize his skills as a manager. Free him up for the management challenge instead of burying him in details. 'Knowing what he is responsible for but who is *accountable*,' was another way you put it. And I have seen the same situation developing for the non-management personnel, especially in Job Procedures. Here's where the employee is given the same opportunity to bring to his job station a sort of objectivity. He is encouraged to improve job detail directives. Sure the J.P. may be in existence when he takes the station over, but that doesn't prevent him from bringing his own creativeness to the job and making appropriate changes in the step-by-step detail.

"In this system," I continued, "you have all that is good about participatory management, none of the things that are insidiously bad. The non-management group participates in solving management's problems but does so within the framework of a management designed device or system."

Bob's eyes were sparkling as his awareness of these residual benefits came into clear focus. He designed a system for the administrator, but under the scrutiny of an industrial psychologist it would pass most of the tests he could put to it. The dimensions of the system seemed to be without boundaries. Now I was primed to the degree of excitement to hear about the fourth and last phase of 4BMAP!

How to Take the Sting Out of the Word "Inspection"

"Before we get into it," Bob started, "answer this question. What connotation do you put on the word 'inspection'? Is it a positive or a negative connotation?"

"Negative!" I answered firmly and promptly.

"Most people answer the same way. Isn't that strange? I mean, there are lots of positive aspects to inspections. I, for instance, wouldn't get on an airplane if I didn't know it was inspected. I'd be scared silly of the electric current in my house if I didn't know the system was inspected. There are hundreds of positive inspections that go on every hour and we all thank God they do! Yet ask a man how he reacts to the word 'inspection' and invariably he will say 'negative.' ''

I had no argument to offer so he went on.

"What happens, of course, is this," he said. "He relates the word to himself . . . as though he was the one who is going to be inspected . . . and right away he has a negative reaction. People don't like to be inspected. The word implies, to them, a witch hunt. They are going to be subjected to a scrutiny that might reveal them or annoy them. Instinctively they get defensive.

"If I said to you, 'In one sentence write down on that paper what you think of 4BMAP,' you would write it down. It might be complimentary or it might be critical, but you would write *something*. But if I added at the end of the question, 'I want to inspect your handwriting,' what would you then think? 'My God, he isn't interested in my answer, he wants to see how I write. He wants to inspect my penmanship.' And how will you attack the paper? Very carefully!" he laughed.

"If you are a poor writer, you probably won't give me an answer at all. You will defend your right to tell me to get lost."

Two Types of Inspection

Just for a second he paused, then asked me to visualize a man who runs a machine. "You stand beside him and watch. If he's proficient he will want to show off. If he isn't, he'll be nervous. But let's say he is proficient. Now, suppose we have someone tell him that in an hour the boss is coming to inspect his handling of the machine. Two things are likely to affect his performance. First, he may fear the boss and that will account for his nervousness. But second, if he doesn't fear the boss as a *person,* he will fear the *concept* of the inspection, and *that* will make him nervous!"

He stared at me as though he was savoring a delicious morsel! "Now, try to imagine a system which makes the man *want* to be inspected—makes him angry if he isn't inspected—

makes him look forward to being told that he is *going* to be inspected. Wouldn't that be quite a system?"

"Yes, almost unbelievable, I would say," I remarked.

"Well, you can sure believe it! It's called the 'Detailed Job Inspection' system—D.J.I. for short—and when it is introduced and functioning the word 'inspection' loses all negative connotations. Fantastic, but true!"

"How does it work?" I asked impatiently.

How Inspections Are Frequently Conducted

"Well, let me tell you how it came into my mind first. Many years ago I was a flunky in a plant. One day we were all told that the general manager was coming out on his annual inspection. I saw the bosses go out of their trees getting things ready. The place looked like a bandbox! Even the handrails shone! Everyone was told what to be doing when Mr. Big arrived—told what to say to him if he stopped to talk. Supervisors were half nuts anticipating things he might look at!

"Well, the day came," he went on. "Mr. Big entered the plant, started his tour, shook hands with as many hands as he could reach without interfering with production, asked questions like 'How do you like your job?', rarely waited for an answer, and in five minutes he was off the floor drinking coffee with the plant manager. A complete waste of time . . . a *laugh*! And believe me, the guys laughed like mad. Foremen were angry and supervisors were livid—all that preparation for nothing.

"I never forgot that. I especially couldn't forget how the foremen and second level managers reacted. They were nearly violent on one hand but happy to see him out of there on the other. The G.M. was a laughable person from the standpoint of the personnel, and I swore right then that if I ever found myself doing an inspection of anyone, it would sure be different from that!"

How the Inspection Method Could Be Improved

"What really was wrong?" I asked. "Isn't that the way most senior inspections are made?"

"Quit asking two questions at a time," he laughed. "First, it was wrong because it was meaningless. A waste of everyone's time. So artificial it was a joke! He didn't inspect a thing . . . and damn it, we were *ready* for an inspection! We had prepared! That's what made the bosses angry. They had shoved the group around to get ready for it and nothing happened. *They* were the ones who had egg all over their faces. Do you think after that experience they could say nice things about senior management? To save their own faces they just made sport of the 'guys upstairs.'

"As for the second question, *yes,* that is the way senior manager inspections are done today. They take a little time to learn. Mind you, up until very recently I doubt if any of them would have any way of comparing *their* inspection methods with correct inspection methods. They would, with hardly an exception, do what their predecessors did—and their predecessors did before them."

"Like the young bride," I added, "who told her husband to cut the shank off the ham. 'Why should I do that?' he asked. 'I don't know; mother always did. Maybe the meat is no good at that end.' 'Phone your mother,' he said. 'Ask her.' She did, and when she came back to the kitchen, she said, 'Mother doesn't know. Grandma always did it. She's phoning grandma now.' In a few moments the phone rang. 'What did grandma say, mother?' There was a pause. 'Oh, I see. The roasting pan in those days was too small for the shank of the ham!' "

Bob laughed at the illustration, then continued. "So it is with most presidents, vice-presidents and general managers. Big fanfare, in they come and out they go and nothing is inspected. If they knew how they were laughed at after they left a plant or a branch, they would find out how to do an inspection, or not make one at all. Actually, that's what is happening. President receptions are now in vogue. They don't come near the office—just have a reception and invite the management people to it. In this way nobody kids anyone. No primping and priming and no time lost. They leave the inspection bit to sub-managers."

Bob poured another cup of coffee and put on his sweater. "Well, that's why I worked out a system for a proper inspection routine," he continued. "There's no way in today's complex production maze for a senior manager to fully understand every nut and bolt of an operation. He must have a working knowledge of most things but he must be able to put his finger on references from which he can get detailed knowledge if he needs it."

Why the Inspector Needs to Be as Prepared as the "Inspected"

"That's the nub of what's wrong with inspections as they are so often done. The work force is prepared for the inspection but the *inspector* isn't. He doesn't know what specific questions to ask . . . doesn't know what areas of a plant to inspect, whom to talk to, and what to listen for in a conversation. The result? He flits around like a butterfly not knowing which flower to land on. He never gets into real detail, but he thinks he does. That's why he gets so little honey and pollinates so damn few buds—just to stretch the analogy to the breaking point!"

We both laughed.

"Instead of seeking information," he went on, "he tries to build a 'nice guy' image. Instead of asking a man what he does, he asks him how he feels. Most men respond to *that* question. But even if he asks him what he does, and gets an answer, his reply is likely to be 'That's fine.' He won't understand a thing the man says. The question was meaningless. Since he really doesn't know what the guy does, he's afraid to show his ignorance by pursuing the point. So 'How do you like the new washroom?' is likely to come out next."

How to Get Response from the Man Inspected

"For example," he illustrated, "let's take the president of a printing plant. He's the president but he's never run a bigger press than a copy machine. He has a craftsman who does that for him. Now, does that mean he shouldn't ever inspect the big five-unit rotary down in the basement? Of course it doesn't. But how can he inspect if if he knows nothing about it? He inspects what he does know about it and what he *should* know about it."

"What's that?" I asked.

"Well, I guess he should know that it's being maintained, right? He has issued maintenance instructions—or his foreman has—and maintenance forms are kept. So he can look at these maintenance instructions right in the plant. That's one thing he can inspect. He may look at these along with the pressman. Safety regulations is another. Housekeeping another. Now they *both* know they are right. Is there something about the press he would like to know? Who better to ask than the pressman? Do you think the pressman isn't going to be happy to teach him? You can bet money on it. There would be dozens of things around that press that he could inspect or should inspect."

"Sure," I said. "But he probably has more important things to do."

"Of *course* he has, and what does that tell you about what he should do? He should set down his priorities. All inspections must be consistent with the time available and the priorities in existence. Perhaps he may go near that press only once a year, but when he *does* he should be prepared. He should be working to a prepared list of questions of inspection points. The list should have spaces between each question so he can make notes. And if he makes notes he should leave a copy of his list and comments for the man inspected. Nothing is covered up. If he makes a complimentary notation the employee reads it; if uncomplimentary, he reads that too."

"Isn't that a lot of work?" I asked.

"That's the wrong question to ask," he said. "The only question to ask is 'Are inspections worthwhile?' If you answer that affirmatively, then this is the only way to carry out the inspection. If your answer is negative, you will be overlooking a really positive way to bridge the gap between management and the work force . . . the only way to get close to the people and let them get close to you. Here's what I mean:

With the Right System, Employees Insist on Inspections

"I asked you how you would like an inspection system in operation that the work force wanted—indeed, demanded. Well, the D.J.I. system is the one. Why? Because its purpose is made clear right from the time it is introduced, and its purpose is to permit management to be fully informed, ask intelligent questions, so that the work force can respond, can be heard, can show off their expertise or show off their problems. And that's the best kind of boss/worker relationship."

The Opportunity to Show Talent

He paused to light a cigarette. As he inhaled he said, "So often we think the little guy down on the press, on the bench or assembly line or in the truck or at the desk, just does what he's told to do—hasn't an original thought in his mind—isn't proud of the talent he has or the job he does. That's nonsense! That sure doesn't square with the most simple definition of a human being. I've never met a man or a woman who doesn't want to strut his stuff to anyone who's interested and intelligent enough to appreciate the talent behind the stuff. What's the good of talent if you can't show it off? Why do we have movie stars? Do you think they could be convincing in their dramatizations if the only people they could show their talents to were limited to the one they see in the mirror? It's part of the whole principle of incentive—a big part; some experts are saying the *only* part—being appreciated for showing the talent you have and the way you use it, and your friend Maslow is only one of the experts. But a good one!"

"It sounds great, Bob," I said, "But aren't you assuming that the inspection will always produce some complimentary comment? Suppose it's loaded with criticism?"

"Well, that brings up the only *good* thing about the G.M.'s visit and really accentuates the *bad* thing about most inspections." He swung his feet onto the floor and fixed his attention directly on me. "Remember I told you about being told long in advance about the G.M.'s inspection visit? That gave us time to prepare—to shine the place up—to be coached on what to say in response to questions, etc?"

"Yes, but you said that was artificial nonsense," I interrupted.

"It was! Pure artificiality!" replied Bob. "But the principal wasn't wrong. Pre-notice is not wrong. What makes it artificial is the way managers had to *guess* where the inspection points would be, guess what questions the G.M. might ask. That's a tough exercise in itself. Builds pretty high levels of frustration. Suppose they guess wrong!"

"Well, isn't it an artificial inspection if everyone knows the inspection points and the questions?" I insisted.

"Not if the inspection points are sufficient to make the inspection itself meaningful. That's where the witch hunt idea came from. No one knew what was going to be inspected so everyone approached the inspection as though it was a trap, designed to catch you with your finger in the cookie jar. Its underlying intent appeared to be 'Find reasons to fire people.' Why would a company do something that would create *that* impression? It costs thousands of dollars to hire and train people. Is it conceivable that management would be looking for reasons to fire them? Of course not! Yet that's the impression the average employee gets when you tell him an inspection is going to take place.

**Two Essential Ingredients of
Inspection Success**

"But I'm still not satisfied," I queried. "If you tell the man the inspection points *and* the questions, how do you know you haven't made an inspection of a well-rehearsed act or job performance?"

"The answer can be given in two words—'adequate' and 'frequent.' If your inspection points are adequate to cover the entire job station, what else is there to inspect? And if the inspections are made *often* enough the act or performance you mention will soon become a habit or a pattern."

"But we agreed a minute ago," I said, "that the printing company president didn't have time to make a lot of inspections of the press. How does that square with 'frequent'?"

"It squares perfectly," he smiled knowingly. "Why should the president make *frequent* inspections of the press when he has a superintendent who *lives* in the plant. He's the one who looks after the frequency, and if he's got a well-thought-out inspection list he will be the one to cover the 'adequate' part of the formula."

"Well, does the plant superintendent tell his staff when and how he's going to make inspections?" I asked.

"Of course he does. Everyone who is likely to be inspected knows when and how. I tell my district managers when I'm going to inspect their plants. Not only that, they have a copy of my inspection points. They know exactly what areas I'm going to inspect."

"Do you inspect all areas every time?" I queried.

"No, I can't possibly cover them all on one inspection."

"Then isn't the element of surprise still there? If you have 25 inspection points and you can only inspect five at a time, does he know which five?"

"More or less he does," he affirmed. "He has copies of my previous D.J.I.'s with my comments written on them. He knows I'm not likely to inspect something I inspected the last time, if it was O.K."

**How to Prevent an Inspection from
Turning into a "Witch Hunt"**

"Won't he let those things you're not likely to inspect go unattended?" I insisted.

"There you go with the witch hunt idea again! Gad, is that concept ever imbedded! My inspection points are for the good of the man, the district and myself. In my case, I want to find the roadblocks where my authority is the one to fix it. I'm not looking for errors, I'm looking for proficiency and questions on problems. What I want to see is exactly the same things *he* wants to have happen. He is striving for improvements, not looking for excuses. I inspect nothing that he himself doesn't want to see working with maximum proficiency. And believe me, because he has my list he has a pretty good idea of my own management desires and goals. Usually they are dead-on with *his* because we probably set them together during a Project Committee session."

Bob paused in contemplation, then, "Many times I've gone out on a D.J.I. and have had the man I'm inspecting draw my attention to something that isn't going so well. I had no intention of checking that particular thing until he drew it to my attention. Now do you think he was intentionally exposing himself to criticism? He *wants* some answers! That's why he reveals it. And if I can't give him the answer right then or as soon as I get back to my office, you can be sure that the problem will be brought up in the next P.C. meeting."

How to Overcome an Inspection Dilemma

"Aren't you talking about the inspection of a pretty highly motivated, well-paid manager? Would you expect the rank and file to respond the same way?" I asked.

"I'm letting you answer that question, Gordon. You're the man who studies Maslow and the boys! What would *their* answer be?"

Bob had me in the ringed corner. I was face-to-face with

the kind of doubt that besets every manager who ever gave a thought to psychological theory and its practical application. Can you expect the same response from a worker as you can from a manager when you examine both as human beings? From my own research I knew we were into a highly complex area ... one that I was sure 4BMAP was not intentionally designed for ... and yet, from my examination of the other parts of the system I was pretty convinced that it would cover it accidently if *not* intentionally.

Maslow's theory of need fulfillment was not, in my opinion, wrong. Yet, now that it was under a solid practical test, I was wavering. No wonder managers have their hands full, I thought. Those who don't study the psychology of motivational management are not one bit different than those who do and then fail to apply it. Would a worker respond the same way as a manager? He *should* but *would* he? I wanted more time and more information, and I couldn't get more practical information than what I would get from Bob. He was the one who put it to the test, so I resolved to make him answer the question.

"Bob, I have my own opinions, but I'm not sure they are right. Knowing the complexities of theory versus application, I would say from a *theory* point of view the worker *should* respond the same way as a manager. But from a practical point of view, I'm not sure he would and I know there are no 'absolutes.' People vary in their response so dramatically that I doubt if a 'yes' or 'no' answer can be given. About all anyone could be expected to do is try it out. You have done that for quite a number of years, so what is your answer?"

The Answer to the Dilemma

"Maybe I'm a little less cautious than I should be, but for my money, the response is exactly the same possibly ten times more often than it's different."

"Do you think *you* as a manager have anything to do with it?" I asked.

"It's a good point but I don't think it's valid. All of my

sub-managers use this system and they report the same reaction as my own. In companies where I have no influence whatsoever but where the system has been installed, I get no report that is different. You stated yourself, or you quoted a couple of experts, that there is little difference basically between what makes one human being, say, happy and what makes another human being happy."

He was trying to bring an example into his mind. He thought hard for a moment. "Let's go back to the inspection of the press," he said finally. "Do you think the human being, the craftsman, handling that press isn't as fundamentally interested in displaying his expertise as, say, the plant superintendent?"

"Bob, so help me, I know he *should* be as interested, but like every manager in existence I find myself wondering whether he *would* be," I answered truthfully.

"It is very difficult," I continued, "for me to get out of my mind the fact that the pressman is probably part of a big union. All he knows is that he comes to work at 8:00 a.m., pushes buttons, loads the inkwell and watches the mouth of the press spit out the finished product. And for *that* he gets paid, and looks forward to the next bargaining session when he'll get paid some more for doing even less work."

"Well, of course, I cannot discuss the mind of a press-man. . . ."

"You're *escaping*!" I interrupted. "You're drawing some very *wide* exceptions. The theory of a human being's response is not acceptable if we start eliminating a wide cross-section of the human spectrum. The craftsman on the press should not be different from the craftsman on a telephone pole if the theory is correct."

"The theory is correct!" he thumped the arm of the chair. "I won't except out a single craftsman now that you have put me up to it. But I'll tell you what I *will* except out . . . the manager who handles the craftsman. I know that psychiatrists talk about stimulus and response, and response is directly related to stimulus so I'm on safe ground when I say this. So I will tell you that the stimulus of a manager is what affects and controls the response of the employee. Don't look to the employee to explain the different responses, look to the manager!"

"And, on your experience," I pressed on, "using, say, the techniques of the Detailed Job Inspection System, you have come to the conclusion that the manager can predictably get the response that is desired?"

"Yes, definitely. And not just on my experience. On the experience of everyone who uses the system," he said with conviction.

"Bob, you laid the stimulus responsibility on the manager; don't you think the union leadership has to share it pretty substantially?"

The Role of Labor Representatives

"Yes, I most certainly do. As leaders they assume an authoritarian role. Certainly as authorities they stimulate and get a corresponding response. I've been involved with union organizers and bargainers for years. I know their tactics, their strategies, their battle plans and techniques. I'm not convinced or enamored by them any more than you are. And I agree, it is fundamentally wrong to lay the blame of worker response on any other stimulus than what he gets from his managers *or* his union leaders!"

"Well," I said, "the workers don't have too much choice in the managers they get but they have a lot of choice in the union leaders they get, so if they are being conditioned to respond in a way that is psychologically not good for them, why do they vote in the kind of leadership they are getting. They *must* agree with it and therefore I think they *must* assume responsibility for their responses."

"That's like saying a grade two student must be responsible for passing a university exam in higher mathematics. How can he be responsible for something he knows nothing about?" His tone was friendly but pretty crisp!

"Hellsafire," he continued, "We have managers by the

thousands who are not trained in understanding the psychological nuances of management. I don't know a damn thing about it myself but I *feel* it."

"You underestimate yourself! There are few managers who have investigated this whole concept as much as you have."

How Common Sense Plus Experience
Equals Management Effectiveness

"Well, I'm a long way from being an expert. If I have any expertise at all it is just plain common sense plus some tough lessons learned over the years. And one of those lessons I learned was that managers, by doing stupid things, by having no system to work with, are the laughingstocks of many of their employees. They think they are immune from the workers' examination just because they are managers . . . like some kind of divine right . . . but they aren't. That divine right went out with the horseless carriage. Today, half the young workers and many of the older ones have more formal education than many of their managers. The young ones particularly have been raised in an environment of questions, not one of obedience . . . *blind* obedience. They can spot a weak manager a mile away. They know a bluff from an order. They know fear when they see it. Jeepers, they can *smell* fear, and there are managers all over this country who are scared silly, and they're scared primarily because they don't really know what to do. They don't manage their jobs! Their jobs manage them!"

Bob was intensely serious. The depth of his conviction radiated like heat waves from a blast furnace. He was obviously angry at the overall incompetence of management. He seemed to regard the union as a prickly thorn placed in the backside of management *by* management!

The Essential Element

"Certainly I don't know why the workers vote in the leadership that they do," he continued, "but I don't blame them for voting in *someone.* As I said before, management has abdicated its right to lead the men. That was turned over to the union. Management still controls the purse strings, the markets, the production decisions, and well it should, but it has become so preoccupied with these things it has forgotten what it means to *manage!* Manage!—it starts with MAN. If we don't deal with the MAN, we don't deal with the right force at all!

"You will agree," he plowed right on, "that a basically sound psychological principle defines 'happiness' as pursuing a goal which an individual thinks is worthwhile, using his maximum talents. Right?"

"Right!"

"O.K., let's break it down. Let's talk about the pressman again. Does he want happiness?"

"Well, it sounds pretty basic but I would say he can be presumed to want happiness. Most sane people do," I answered.

"Don't be condescending; of course people want happiness, sane or insane. If happiness is the pursuit of a goal which an individual thinks worthwhile and he is given the chance to utilize his maximum talents, can you honestly believe that a pressman is going to go contrary to the principle and intentionally do those things that will make him unhappy?"

"Not intentionally," I said. "But unintentionally, I'll bet he is doing exactly that."

"You're right!" Bob exclaimed. "That's exactly the reason we have so much labor unhappiness, discontent, friction, tension and every other word that describes a condition called 'unhappiness.' The vast majority of the workers in this country are *unintentionally* moving in exactly the wrong direction. They've been caught in the trap of following a leader who is himself going in the wrong direction."

"Are you talking about the labor leader?"

"Of course I am," he said.

"Just a minute ago you gave me the impression that all of the ills with manpower were the responsibility of the manager, you know, MANager? It begins with MAN!" I was being a bit facetious.

"And I don't withdraw. They *do* begin with management. As I said, management got so critically tied up with the bigger problems of corporate growth and profitability it abdicated its rights to *manage* . . . you know . . . it begins with MAN?" More sarcasm!

"So," I said, "while management made the mistake of abdicating its man-management responsibilities, what you are saying is that the union leader who picked up the responsibility is botching it just as much."

How "More Pay for Less Work" Should Be Analyzed

"Precisely," smiled Bob. "You're getting the message. The union's general philosophy is 'More pay for less work.' There are dozens of component parts to that philosophy that are in that fast summation. Yet, if there is any philosophy that is more diametrically opposite to that definition of happiness we agreed to, I don't know what it is."

The Problem of Leisure

"How come? Maybe a guy is happier doing less and getting more. Maybe he finds his happiness outside of his work," I challenged.

"Go ahead, give me some examples," he taunted right back.

"Maybe he likes to go to the beach and do nothing."

Bob laughed out loud! "You don't mean that. You have only to look at what happens to thousands of people who retire to know that won't make them happy for long. As soon as they stop pursuing a goal (retire) they start withering and dying . . . and with thousands of 67-year olds, they actually do die. You've got to come up with an illustration better than that!"

"O.K., maybe he wants to pursue a hobby. He needs more time to do it. If he gets more pay and has more time *too* he should be very happy," I responded.

"And he would be," he smiled, "but there isn't a single statistic in existence that says everyone pursues a hobby that will fulfill the equivalent of a day's work. In fact, one of the most difficult problems facing this country is finding out what people can do with their leisure time. In the last decade this has become a national and a critical challenge. Too much time on our hands. My mother used to say, 'Time spent in idleness is time spent in planning trouble!'—and if there is any relationship between the fantastic expansion of crime and the expansion of time, I guess mother was right! Idle time does seem to be spent in planning trouble. It may not mean crime though. It can mean anything from being fed up with a spouse, a child or a neighborhood and making changes, to being bored to the point of a neurosis. And here again, if there is any relationship between the expansion of leisure time and the expansion of mental illness, maybe we should be taking a hard look at that!"

"Maybe a guy would just like to read a lot more," I said trying to stagger into an illustration he *couldn't* shoot down.

"Not valid at all. There has been no time when we had more reading material available at lower costs than we have now. But you aren't likely to find any substantial improvement in reading habits. Educationalists are saying the same things about the public's reading habits today that they said 50 years ago. And if more reading *is* done, I'll just bet my last dollar that it is 'escape reading.' And if that doesn't tell you something, it should."

"O.K., Bob," I said, defeated for the moment. "You're winning. More pay for less work is not a good principle to apply if happiness is the desired result. The union leadership is botching things up pretty well. And of course that brings me back to why do the workers elect those leaders?"

How Managers Have Grown Less Effective

"Because," he answered gleefully, "they have not found the leadership they want and need in management. Again, MANagement!"

"Bob," I said rather aggressively, "you continue to emphasize the MAN part of management. Doesn't management *really* do a lot of MANagement? I mean, have we ever had a time in our history when management was doing *more* for the MAN? We've got a veritable cradle-to-grave welfare concept in most companies . . . sickness plans, holiday plans, pensions . . . and if management has missed anything, the government has provided it, and you will certainly admit that management is paying the tab in taxes. How much *more* attention can management *give* to the worker?"

"Good heavens, Gordon, are you telling me that because management supplies a bunch of fringe benefits . . . most of which were forced on them by unions . . . they are MANaging?" Bob appeared incredulous.

"By the way you ask the question, I had better say 'no' to that! Go ahead. Lay it on me," I laughed.

"Well, I don't want our discussion to degenerate into a debate over labor/management relations. But I must insist that the direct contact that management has with the men it manages has become less and less effective and is directly opposite to the contact the union has and is making, which has become more and more of an influence."

"Are you expecting management to go home with the worker? I mean, how far can this direct contact go?" Now I was getting warm!

"No, I certainly don't expect that management will go home with the worker," he affirmed. "The union leaders don't go home with him, so why should management? What I do expect is that management will look at the employee as an individual . . . that it will apply to the individual some of the fancy theories the psychologists and experts have been espousing these last ten or so years. I admit it is trying to get closer to its work group all the time, but it is still caught up in this handshaking bit. Men don't want their hands shaken. They want to talk to a manager who knows something about the job. They want to be asked meaningful questions. They want to offer appreciated suggestions."

"Well, you admitted that the union leaders don't apply good psychological theory and are botching the men badly . . . ." I couldn't finish my point.

How the Employee Group Recognizes
Effective Leadership

"You're damn right I admitted it," he interjected, "and that's just why I'm so excited about the possibilities. They *have* screwed it up for the man. The men don't know it yet, but they sure will pretty soon. In fact, and mark this well, the rank and file is learning in about the same way and at the same speed as management is learning. The worker is learning that his union leadership is now pursuing a course that is *not* in his best interests as a human being and management is learning that it must assume the responsibility for teaching him the right way, and it can only do that by the example it sets, and it *must* be better than the example the union leaders are setting."

"And the dawn is beginning to break in my thick skull," I admitted. "For a time there I thought you were all union, then I thought you were all management. Now I see you are all *worker*—but you are looking to management, *not* the union, to solve his problems."

"I hadn't thought of it just that way myself, but I guess that's about right. I know that the worker is the very lifeblood of any organization. I know that management should have the responsibility to see that he is properly MANaged. I also know that it abdicated that responsibility for awhile to the unions, and the unions have outserved their real value to the man because they are a mile off the track when it comes to doing what is *really* necessary to make the man a happy human being. And now the worker is getting wise to it . . . management is getting wise . . . and pretty soon all things will be back in order."

How to Find Solutions Rather Than Faults

"And unless I miss my guess," I said, "the Detailed Job Inspection System is one tool that will accelerate management's ability. Right?" I asked.

"Right!" he exclaimed. "Not just ability, but method. That's what has been missing . . . a *method*!"

"And part of the method," I said, "just to get back to where we both came into this discussion, is the pre-announcement of the inspection and the pre-listing of the inspection points."

"I would agree to that, providing pre-announcement and pre-listing means 'frequent' and 'adequate.' *And* that the orientation of the inspector is to find improvement and not fault . . . solutions rather than criticism!"

"Well," I said, "it took me a little time to understand the union/management thing, but I'm still having trouble with pre-announcements and pre-listings."

"And you have lots of company," he laughed. "It goes back to school and university, although, thank God, it is changing. I refer to the surprise exam or the blind exam. Kids don't know when the 'inspection' is coming and have only a vague idea of what they are going to be 'inspected' on. They do a whole year's work and are told they are going to be examined on any part of it. It's almost impossible for them to prepare for it—to study a year's work in a week or two.

"What's the result?" he continued. "They don't really prepare—they try to cram, to memorize. If they knew the questions they were going to be asked and if the number of questions adequately covered the subject for the students to be considered reasonably proficient, then the students would concentrate on those questions and would probably reach the desired level of competence.

"It's the same with D.J.I.'s," he went on. "Pre-announcement removes the surprise factor which isn't appreciated, and the pre-listing informs the 'student' what questions are going to be asked, and more important, informs the manager what subjects he should brush up on himself."

"And that," I said, "is how management can get into a direct meaningful relationship with the staff—right?"

"Right!"

How Senior Management Can Handle
Bench-Level Inspections

"Then answer this question," I taunted. "How will the president of General Motors inspect little ole Bill Smith on the assembly line?"

Bob chuckled. "You still think you have me trapped, don't you?"

"Not at all," I smiled back. "I know better—so go ahead answer me."

"He isn't expected to inspect Bill Smith. . . . "

"Aha!" I exclaimed, "I *have* caught you!"

"You didn't let me finish," he scolded. "He isn't expected to inspect Bill Smith—but the general production manager could do it once every year, the factory manager could do it once every six months, the floor supervisor could do it once a month and the section foreman could do it once a week."

"That sounds like a lot of inspection," I suggested, a bit less aggressively.

"Considering the effort management must make to reclaim the MANagement role it's not nearly *enough*. How often does the union get at the man to 'inspect' him for their purposes? If we expect to reclaim the management function we had better walk through the wall as often as it is possible. Wouldn't you agree?" he asked.

I thought about this for a full minute. Bob sat quietly. As it went through my mental filters it began to make sense. The frequency of the visits made *great* sense. I put silent words to my thoughts. "Management D.J.I.'s are the means and a deeper understanding is the result," I repeated it to myself. Yes, it made a *lot* of sense, but I didn't want to fully declare myself at the moment.

"Well, I must admit," I said, "I'm close to agreeing. I suppose it is the uniqueness of the approach that is hard to get used to. It seems to be the first concrete, yet basically simple technique that has come to the attention of management for decades."

"That's why it's effective," Bob smiled. "It *is* concrete and it is simple. Perhaps too simple to command respect. But I can say this: I don't know a manager who uses D.J.I.'s who won't admit that since he started using them he has experienced a more cooperative and harmonious relationship with his work force.

"As I said at the outset, installed properly, the men *want* the inspections—are annoyed if they aren't inspected—primarily because they are denied the pleasure of showing management what they can do, indicating what they have done, and simply discussing what they hope to do. It's the greatest thing that has ever happened in the file of management/worker relationships."

Who Will Make the Final Choice of the Leader?

"Now comes the $64.00 question," I said, hoping I would really throw a block into him this time. "What are the unions going to do while you proceed to give management the road map back to its proper relationship with the rank and file?"

"I don't think it's a case of what the union will do with it or about it," he answered. "I think it's more a case of what the worker will do about it. He's the final judge. If he sees management doing those things that are really designed to get the *best* out of him, as distinct from the *most,* he will eventually sort out his loyalties."

"By that do you mean he will go against the union?"

"Not at all. He will put his union in the correct perspective. I think it is a permanent fact of life that the union will be around for a long time. And I don't get upset about that one bit. If it acts as a balance in the pendulum swings between the worker and management, I think it contributes to both the worker and management. The union should serve a peace-keeping role. It is a deterrent, so to speak."

"A deterrent against management, though," I reminded him. "Only management will suffer if the union intercedes."

"When the worker has a choice he can be counted upon to vote the right leader in. Now, there is no choice. He thinks the union is all on his side and it boils down to the old theory, 'The devil you know is better than the devil you don't know.' When he gets to know management in a new role, he will change. He will eliminate the labor leader who is just trying to start labor/management wars."

How Workers Will Choose

"Are you sure you're not dreaming a little?" I teased.

"No more than management was dreaming when it didn't think the unions would last or would get control as they have. Management thought it was impregnable. History is loaded with examples of people and nations who thought they were invincible or who thought they were facing invincibility. This is no different. The ranks of management were breached by the unions and now the tables are turning. Slowly, I admit, but exceedingly well."

"The way you put it, Bob," I observed, "is almost like the ways of politics. The fortunes of one party go up just as soon as the fortunes of the other one go down."

"That's right. And the voter makes the final choice. In this case, the worker will make it, and that's who should make it. But today, management's fortunes are slowly rising. I don't mean in dollars and cents, but in acumen, awareness. It has picked up a little knowledge beyond the purview of an assembly line or a new market or production technique. Technological advance won't stop, but it will slow down just long enough to allow management to catch up with the human needs."

"How do you see this in respect to 4BMAP?" I asked.

"4BMAP is nothing more than a system, a tool, to give

expression to the knowledge I referred to. We've had a lot of water go under management's bridge since Taylor first picked up a shovel, or McGregor struck his Theory X and Maslow his Human Needs. Management has been learning for a long time. It just hasn't been applying what it learned as well as it might. But after saying that, may I also say it hasn't had the system to help it. 4BMAP is that system! And I think, since we are coming to the end of this discussion, that I should say something else. Not all companies or all management should be painted with the same brush. We've got many, many exceptions in this country. They enjoy amazingly fine employee relationships. I wouldn't want any reader of yours to get the impression, or be left with the impression, that I have placed all companies in the same category."

It was ten minutes past nine. Except for the brilliance of the stars and the lights in the harbor it was quite dark. Mrs. Babbidge was true to her word. She was standing at the sun deck entrance reminding us that 9:00 o'clock was to have been the deadline!

For the balance of the evening we just chatted . . . family, friends, experiences. Not a mention of what had been going on all day. It was characteristic of my host's methods. One subject was closed and it wasn't going to be reopened until the next day. In effect, office hours were over! Now it was time for relaxation!!

TEN

How you can use 4BMAP as a "full circle" management system

After breakfast Bob took me on a tour of the many channels that make up Huntington Harbour. The sun dazzled us as it bounced around on the water. We went up one channel and down another. The boats in the area were luxurious and I couldn't resist feeling envious of the whole scene. But if anyone was enjoying it, it was Bob. I suppose he had done this tour a few hundred times but his enthusiasm for the boats, the homes, the whole area was typical of his enthusiasm for life itself!

As we tied up at his wharf, sat down on the lounge chairs, I asked him for a windup chapter.

"Give me a summation of it all, Bob. We talked about four distinct phases of a single system. Try to sum it all up for me, O.K.?" I asked.

"Thanks for the invitation. I don't know whether I'm going to sum it up as much as make a couple of clarifications. First, whether you turn this discussion into a pamphlet or a book, your reader will not know anything but the basics of 4BMAP."

"Thanks a lot," I said. "You sure know how to hurt a guy!"

"I don't mean to, but it's like this: As I reflect on our discussions, they have been largely oriented to the *potential* of 4BMAP as distinct from the installation of 4BMAP."

"Run that past me again," I said.

"Well, I have been directed somewhat by your questions to establish the efficacy of the program rather than the methods by which it is installed . . . and *that* is quite a subject by itself," he answered.

"Why? Is it difficult to install it?" I asked.

"No, not difficult at all. It could probably be categorized as simple once the formal instruction is given, and that, in total, takes about 20 hours.

First Steps in Introducing 4BMAP

"During the instruction the managers actually start programming their jobs into the system. They'll write up 15 to 20 P.M.P. items, line up a half a dozen important J.P.'s, write their first O.L., prepare a list of projects to be undertaken, and probably do a rough draft of a D.J.I. list.

"After the instruction they will start programming their entire job into the system. They aren't expected—nor would they be able—to program it all in a couple of weeks. Since they know the system they keep an eye on their job responsibilities and their accountabilities, and they keep adding items, supervising the preparation of Job Procedures, writing Operating Letters whenever they see the need for policy directives or special type instructions. They organize and launch their Project Committees and start introducing and actually doing their Detailed Job Inspections."

"How long would it take a manager to get his entire job programmed?" I asked.

The Manager's Programming Schedule

"How long would it take a manager to get his *entire* job programmed? Hard to say. It depends primarily on the number of responsibilities he has—the component parts of his job function. Instructors encourage the graduate to make an objective of writing up one P.M.P. item every day and overseeing the preparation of one J.P. If the objective is maintained, he will have most of his job and the jobs of his work force into the system in six to eight months—again, depending on his job components and those of his work force. And of course, as new requirements materialize, he adds them to the system."

"Do they work with him in the post instruction period?"

"They haven't found it to be necessary, although they will call them back into the classroom in about three weeks, or go over to their office and hold a meeting there. In that way they can discuss any problems the managers may have run into, straighten out any misunderstandings they have, and from that point on they never turn back."

"In a large company would they teach every manager?" I asked.

"No, as a rule they teach ten or 12 key executives who then teach the subordinate workers. In this way the investment in the installation is kept pretty low because all they are actually purchasing are the instructor and student kits. They supply their own instructors and away it goes," he smiled.

"Is there any point at which they find the installation a bit, shall I say, sticky?" I queried.

"I'm not sure I understand 'sticky,' but if it means 'reluctance' of the student to use the system, the answer is decidedly 'no'. After he has written his sixth P.M.P. item he starts to tumble and he never stops until he has his job completely programmed, with bases covered he never dreamed possible."

"Is there any way you could briefly describe an installation?" I asked.

"No way at all," he replied. "It's not that I want to make it sound complex or difficult, because it most certainly isn't. However, anything that takes 20 hours . . . and you do intend to catch a plane this afternoon, don't you?" A little sarcasm!

"As I said, you sure know how to hurt a guy!"

We were both laughing when Mrs. Babbidge, overhearing his last remark, let him have a good blast about how to win friends and influence people! It was a welcome interlude of fun!

"O.K.," I pressed on, "what else can you say in summation?"

"Well, I'd rather like to emphasize that because you're a labor relations guy, you led me into discussions and debates about labor/managment. I enjoyed it, mind you, but I sure wouldn't want your readers to get the idea that 4BMAP was in any way designed to give management a system for knocking labor on the head. I started designing this system long before I ever ran into a union."

"Would you believe, long before unions were even invented?" I smiled.

"Now you're the guy who knows how to hurt a guy!" he laughed. "No, it didn't go quite that far back. But it sure went back to the days of company controlled unions when management wasn't as challenged by unions as it is now."

"I was just kidding you, Bob. I know the system was designed to give management an administrative system that would substantially improve its ability to apply its expertise. But as you said, I couldn't help but get involved with the subject of unions, and I must say this—I'm delighted with the way the system has the potential of bringing to management's attention many things that could improve labor/management relationships."

"Well, I'm not apologizing for that," he replied, "but I must say again, it just happened to turn out that way."

"That's hard to believe, Bob. It may not have had anything to do with labor in the beginning but it seems to reflect so closely those theories and beliefs about management's responsibility that you espoused in this discussion that I can't help thinking it was custom designed to give expression to those exact theories."

"If you want to think that, be my guest. It doesn't hurt my feelings to be made to look like an expert theoretician on labor/management problems. But if you don't clarify my *real* feelings and those of Pence Dacus in that book, I . . . I . . . I'll fix you, I won't even buy a copy of it!"

How to Explain, Introduce, Execute, Supervise and Inspect

"O.K., I'll clarify it," I said laughing at his modesty, "but my reader's opinion is something else. What other summation can you make?"

"Well, you may think this is a prejudiced statement," he replied, "but I can say it with conviction based on experience. The 4BMAP system is the only full circle management system in existence!"

"What does full circle mean?" I asked.

"You can start at almost any phase of the system and it will bring into focus all the other phases.

"For instance, suppose a manager decides to issue a directive to his work force. Let's keep it simple and say the directive involves the policy of the company in relationship to overtime. He uses the Operating Letter System to send out this directive.

"In the O.L. he starts off by giving a brief outline of the purpose. This tells *why*. He then outlines the policy in an item description. This tells them *what* the policy will be. Next, what forms are to be used, *how* they are to be used, *when* they are to be sent, *who* is responsible and what is to be done with them.

"Now that the policy is revealed and the broad outlines of what, how, who and when are indicated, he can post his item of responsibility into his own Planned Management Program . . . his P.M.P. This outlines 'who' is going to do 'what' and 'when' and 'how' he himself must perform to see that it is done.

"He can then write up a Job Procedure or have a subordinate do it, or give it to the person who will be handling the overtime job station. This will tell him or her what to do when overtime claims are made. Subordinate managers can have J.P.'s written for their own personnel so they know how to make an application for overtime.

"The manager wants to keep his finger on the overtime costs so he adds another inspection point on his Detailed Job Inspection list. With this he can spot problems with overtime as fast as they occur. If he spots a problem and hasn't got a solution for it, he has a Project Committee to take it to. If they come up with a solution, he would probably introduce it with another Operating Letter . . . full circle.

How the Project Committee Solves a Problem
and What Happens to the Solution

"Here's another illustration," he went on.

"Suppose he has an item on his P.M.P. that says he must review a small tool inventory report every third month. On this occasion he finds quite a difference between the current report and the previous one. He adds this item to his D.J.I. list because he wants to do an on-site inspection. When he goes to the site and makes his inspection, he'll leave the new D.J.I. list with his foreman. In that way the foreman will always know that the boss might inspect the small tool inventory report.

"Anyway, he discusses the item with the foreman, or whoever is in charge, and they discover they have a theft problem. What's the solution? It doesn't have one at that exact moment.

"It's introduced as a project at the next P.C. meeting. Someone is put in charge of the project. They do some investigating and find the thefts are due to kids hanging around the workshop. Solution? Keep kids out of the workshop—I'm keeping it simple! Out go instructions in an Operating Letter.

P.M.P.'s for follow-up of the instructions are recorded. Some-body prepares a Job Procedure on workshop security, and the job is done, quickly, orderly and effectively.

How Management Directives Can Be "Locked In"

"How about this one," he continued. "Take a typical management meeting. The boss hands out assignments. People take notes. They go back to their job stations and find no place to start on the assignment given—no place to even keep track of it.

"For instance, the boss says, 'From now on I want each of you to give me a report on your department's production every month.'

"The notes are made and the man arrives back at his job station. What's he going to do? Transfer the note to the calendar pad? That looks after this month. What is the guy going to use for the rest of the year?

"Nine times out of ten that boss will get production reports from about 80% of his team during the first month. Then it drops.

"In three months he will be lucky to get one out of five. Then what happens? A bunch of department heads get roasted by one angry boss!

"With this system, the department head goes back to his office, writes up a P.M.P. and has someone prepare J.P.'s for those who are accountable for the guts of the report, makes sure there is enough time for the report to be made up; and he has it every month as requested—on time, done as he wants it done, when and how, and he doesn't even have to remember to do it.

"Again, that's what I mean by full circle," he continued. "It's a complete management system. It doesn't matter what comes up, there is a place for it. If it's a management responsibility it goes into a P.M.P.; if it's non-management it goes into a J.P.; if it's a directive to subordinates, it can go on an O.L.; if it's a problem it can go to the P.C.; and if it requires on-the-spot follow-ups it can go onto a D.J.I. list!

"It's effective, complete in its concept and simple in its application." He paused, smiled broadly and finished with, "Great, eh!"

"It's fascinating, Bob," I asserted. "It really is! It *is* a full circle management system. I can see that no matter where you cut into it, it has enough system within it to carry everything to a completion point. In fact, as I see it, there isn't a thing a manager can face that cannot be effectively introduced into the system. Not only introduced, but followed up by *what, how, who* and *when.*

Some of the Expertise That Went into 4BMAP

"O.K.," said Bob. "You're sold. Now there's one final thing I want to say. I felt all through our discussions that you had the idea that I was the only one responsible for the development of the 4BMAP system. I'm not; I had a lot of help."

I tossed paper and pencil in the air. "For gosh sakes, why didn't you say so earlier?" I asked, surprised and a bit miffed.

"Now don't get sore. Let me explain it very carefully so that no one gets any misunderstandings." He cleared his throat, smiled, and went on. "Here's what happened. First, I created a follow-up system for myself which is now called P.M.P. I used it strictly to help me go through the various job functions. It was pretty crude to begin with, and as time went on I got the rest of the managers started. Gradually, I built the J.P., O.L., P.C. and D.J.I. systems. They were very elemental and by brute strength, determination, and particularly authority, I pushed them into existence and use by my work group. They weren't polished methods by any stretch of the imagination but they worked for me and the group and that was all I cared about."

"You mean it was the 4BMAP system but not with the 4BMAP name?"

Evolution of the System

"Pretty well. It certainly didn't have a name, and it was so basic it didn't contain anywhere near the present 4BMAP system, so there weren't any training techniques. They were just introduced by my constant pushing and adamant attitude. I simply wanted to have a system that would look after Bob Babbidge. I never trained anyone. In fact, there wasn't any training element built into the system then. I didn't see my system as ever being anything that was *teachable,* if you know what I mean. I suppose it boils down to the fact that I didn't even recognize it as a *system* for many years. It was nothing more than a routine that I, Bob Babbidge, used to keep Bob Babbidge's shop out of trouble!"

"Well, how did it ever get to be the system that it is now?" I asked with a little disappointment in hearing him put it down as being strictly a one-man effort to keep himself out of trouble!

"That was more by accident than anything else. In fact, if it hadn't been for Dr. Pence W. Dacus, there would be no 4BMAP, no system especially designed for instruction and introduction to companies. Pence heard me lecture about management systems at a business seminar and later he invited me over to his office to discuss it in more detail. At the time he was the Dean of Continuing Education at Pepperdine University in Los Angeles, which was growing rapidly and needed good management administration. By working together and developing as we went along, we introduced the systems into his shop. It worked so well we decided to try some seminars for local businessmen.

The First Seminar

"In fact, our first seminar was on P.M.P. only. By this time the name 'P.M.P.' had materialized. We developed the P.M.P. instructional material as the class was actually in progress. As time went on we named each of the systems within 4BMAP, and wrote four textbooks. By the time we knew we had something good that would really benefit everyone. We needed a real group of professionals to help us package it into instructor kits, self-instruction kits, seminar kits, etc., and we got them. Pro's in writing, organizing, layout, art, legal matters, accounting, consultants, you name it, and we got them. Of course Pence was a real 'pro,' and while I'm really a modest guy at heart, I am no slouch either. We had a real team!

"As I think back on those days I never cease to wonder at the enthusiasm and the dedication of these people. They just seemed to get caught up in the excitement of this new discovery and they haven't stopped. We still kill most Saturdays with meetings.

"Inevitably, the market potential of the whole system and others we are developing became pretty exciting so we formed a company called Promanent International Inc., and I would think, as things have mushroomed during the last two and a half years, that we have quite a potential."

"Yes, I would think you are right," I said, to let him take a breath. "Does Promanent do the teaching or is it still done in Pepperdine?"

"Oh, it's being taught by qualified instructors working with Promanent, and by Pepperdine. While I can't identify the colleges or universities by name, because contracts have not been signed, I would say that before 1974 is finished, there will be at least six other colleges or other institutions teaching 4BMAP and Promanent will have representatives in half a dozen major cities and in two or three countries!"

**How the Independent Businessman,
Professional, Etc., Can Use the System**

"Do Promanent instructors hold seminars regularly now?" I asked.

"Only when a company commissions them to do so. They

don't have open seminars as such, although they may do that in time. Right now they work with companies or organizations."

"In other words, an individual businessman is not able to take the course without his company sponsoring him?" I asked.

"Not entirely. There are many small businessmen who do not have the personnel to justify holding a seminar. They can take 4BMAP through a self-instruction kit or the business school at Pepperdine University. We designed this method just to take care of those who for one reason or another cannot attend a seminar."

"Have many individuals taken advantage of it?" I asked.

"Actually, few individuals even know it exists," he answered. "It keeps them pretty busy looking after their corporate clients without actively soliciting the small business-man. But they have started promoting the self-instruction kits and have 50 or 60 graduates to date."

"Well, who would be likely to be interested in the self-instruction kit?" I asked.

"I would think every doctor and dentist would be interested. Every grocer, druggist, service station operator, self-employed insurance agent, lawyer, realtor, shop keeper, engineer. Any individual who is conducting a business that requires him to do any amount of administration should be interested."

How a University Professor Became an Efficient Property Manager

He went into his briefcase and came up with a three-ring binder. "Here's a P.M.P. put together by a university professor. Now you would wonder how a professor could use a P.M.P. Well, in this case, he uses it not only on his job as a professor, but also to keep his little business under control. He owns and rents nine houses in L.A. Before he started using 4BMAP he was forgetting to renew the insurance; forgetting to maintain the equipment in the houses, lawn mowers, swimming pools furnaces, etc.; forgetting to pay the taxes until he was into penalties. His little business was turning into a big headache. Not anymore. He goes through his P.M.P. binder checking each item once a week and he misses nothing. More than that, he never gives his business a thought from one week to the other. He knows everything is in the system and he lets the system do the work of remembering for him. When something new comes up he just adds it into the system."

Bob opened the book to the J.P. section. "Here's a complete rundown listing things to do when he overhauls a lawn mower. Here's a J.P. on maintaining a furnace. Look at this one. It tells him exactly what steps to follow in buying a house ... the escrow regulations, conveyancing, financing, everything. Can you see him buying a house now without remembering every single detail? It's like a check list. He made it out once and he doesn't have to think about it again."

"You know, I can see 4BMAP in the average home," I observed. "I'd hate to tell you how I maintain my own home. I think the principle I use is, 'When something goes wrong, fix it.' Of course I don't know how to fix anything, but with a J.P. carefully prepared, maybe my son could do it!"

We both chuckled. Bob got up and I knew I had been given the signal for terminating the interview. It was near flight time and it was an hour's drive to the airport.

As I shook hands I said, "Bob, you have been a gracious host. Your good wife has been a jewel. Between the information you have given me and the hospitality you have shown me, I'm leaving L.A. a very delighted and informed individual. I think I *will* write the book."

"If it isn't too expensive I'll buy one," was his parting comment.

As I walked down the long passageway the only words that ricocheted around my head were, "I'll be back!" How right those words turned out to be.

ELEVEN

Five important observations based on experiences

217

Since the interview, I have had the opportunity to work with a number of companies that have installed the 4BMAP system. The experience has clarified a number of questions that lingered in my mind after interviewing Bob.

You Need Have No Fear of
Pre-Announcing Inspections

As you recall, I had some misgivings about the "pre-announcement" of inspection times and inspection points.

In the instruction and installation programs I have conducted or witnessed to date, my misgivings have proven to be groundless. Pre-announced inspection dates are appreciated by work forces. They obviously eliminate the "witch hunt" concept most employees have in their reaction to an inspection. Since no one is going to be put on the spot, the inspections are done in a climate of mutual respect and positive orientation. And since the perimeters of the inspection are clearly defined for the employee, he senses quickly that management is really interested in his job station and in him as an individual.

When the system is correctly introduced he knows that the inspection is a two-way street, that he will have ample opportunity to point out his problems as well as demonstrate his abilities. He also knows that his suggestions are going to be listened to and acted upon. And since he keeps a copy of the inspector's comments, he knows exactly what's on record.

I suppose the greatest part of it lies in the fact that he knows management hasn't forgotten him; that he belongs, has an important role to play, and is being asked for his opinions and suggestions.

How Inspections Can Win Men Back to You

I must go on record and support Bob Babbidge in his comments about some managers forfeiting their rights to manage men and, through default, finding this part of their responsibility being taken over by union leaders.

I'm satisfied that it may take a generation of workers to permit management the privilege of re-establishing a meaningful type of face-to-face relationship with workers at large. But I'm also satisfied that the Detailed Job Inspection system is the first step—and I think that's all management requires.

You Can Have Multiple Numbers of Project Committees

As for the multiplicity of Project Committees, no evidence reveals this to be a problem. In the large companies, having clearly defined management levels, the system can work at all levels. In the smaller or medium-sized companies it will probably work at the senior staff level only, but that is not to say that even line managers cannot or do not have their own Project Committees.

Even School Taxes Might Be Lowered
Because of 4BMAP

Since the original manuscript was written for this book, the 4BMAP program has captured the interest of a number of school administrators. The efficacy of the program in this field is exciting. With school budgets soaring, it behooves the administration to examine closely any system that will reduce confusion, speed up work flow and possibly reduce operating costs. That 4BMAP has the capacity to do this in industry has already been established.

In addition to school systems, hospitals, government offices and corporations, 4BMAP is worthy of the attention of the one-man, one-girl business, sole proprietors of stores, service stations, legal offices, dentists or doctors.

How One General Manager Summed It All Up

As a final comment, I would like to go on record by congratulating the two main authors of the 4BMAP program, Robert F. Babbidge and Dr. Pence W. Dacus. They have made a contribution to administrative science that will rank with the contributions made in all other sciences during this century. While this is purely a personal opinion, I would rate the development of 4BMAP for the businessman in exactly the same category as I rate the discovery of insulin for the diabetic.

I have a clear recollection of a luncheon interview I had recently with the general manager of a small manufacturing business. I'd had the pleasure of installing the 4BMAP system into his plant six or seven months previous to the luncheon.

After my host reviewed some of the rather exciting things that had happened within the framework of his job responsibilities, he said this:

> But those aren't the real benefits of 4BMAP. The real benefit,
> to me at least, is what has happened to me personally. No
> more worry, no more fear, no more night work or weekends

on the job, and most important of all, no more knots in my gut.

A rather basic way to put it, you will agree, but still and all, a good description of a system that is, itself, basic at the gut level of management effectiveness.